GRACE NOTES

. . .

Also by LAURA GEORGAKAKOS

. . .

Wild Discovery

Billy Graham: God's Ambassador

The Words We Left Unsaid

Grace Notes

Thoughts on Prayer

. . .

Laura Georgakakos

CLUSTER PRESS

THESE LETTERS, ALL ON THE SUBJECT OF PRAYER, were originally written to the leadership of the Community Bible Study class in La Jolla, California. They were sent out weekly from September through May over four consecutive years.

. . .

For

Mary Rumsey
Sister, Shepherd, Teacher, Friend
with love and laughter

...

Year One

...

But as for me, it is good to be near God.
I have made the Sovereign LORD my refuge;
I will tell of all your deeds

—PSALM 73:28

19 SEPTEMBER

Dear Friends,

On Friday I was thinking about God's sovereignty—He is the supreme ruler; He controls all that happens. As I considered whether or not to highlight God's sovereignty in this week's letter, I opened my Bible to Ezekiel 28 and the very first line on the page was, "This is what the Sovereign Lord says…" Halfway down the page the same phrase appeared in Ezekiel 29:3. In verse 13 there it was again. And three verses later, "Then they will know that I am the Sovereign Lord."

Well, clearly **sovereignty** was to be my focus this week! There it was in verse 20 and again seven lines later. On those two pages alone "the Sovereign Lord" appeared eight times. Curious now, I counted my way through Ezekiel. In those 48 chapters the Lord is called "Sovereign" 218 times.

God has all things in hand. When we are feeling close to Him and trust Him, that can be a great relief. But when things aren't going the way we wish we can be frustrated or angry by the fact that He rules and we don't.

How we feel about God's sovereignty—grateful or irritated—can tell us a lot about how yielded we are to Him and His will. It can be a valuable barometer of something needing attention in our relationship. Notice that during those times when we trust in God's unfailing love, we live more peaceably with His sovereignty. This week, set aside what seems to be a more pressing task and intentionally choose to be alone with God. The Sovereign Lord does not rule your life with a fist or a scowl; His hands are open, His arms outstretched. The most amazing truth and gift is this—that the supreme authority and power of the universe, He who controls the motion of the planets and governs the kings of the earth, wants to draw near to you, to sit with you in a comfortable spot to talk and to listen and to laugh. He has things to share, and He longs for your approach.

in Him,

Laura

Sovereign Lord, I get busy and harried and pretend not to hear it, but please keep knocking at the door of my heart. Insist on our time together. Alone with You is where I am supposed to be and I know it. That is the place of greatest blessing and peace; only there will I get the proper perspective on all that is demanding my attention. Thank You for all You are waiting to bestow. *My heart says of you, "Seek His Face!" Your face, LORD, I will seek.* (Psalm 27:8)—Amen.

The LORD would speak to Moses face to face,
as a man speaks with his friend.

—Exodus 33:11

26 SEPTEMBER

Dear Friends,

God wants to speak to us as with a friend. What an amazing prospect! How does a true friend speak to us? Without fear of rejection, freely, honestly, with our best interests in mind. They share their secrets, they ask for our help, they offer their help freely.

Take some time this week to step outside the camp and pitch your tent and be alone with Him. We are aiming to listen and to honestly share as Moses did.

Humor is an important part of sharing with friends. Have you ever had a taste of the Lord's sense of humor? My husband was once on a very long work trip to a remote location in Africa from which it was difficult to make phone calls. I was home with a toddler and greatly looked forward to his calls. I remember praying one morning, "Lord, please let me hear that loved voice today." That afternoon, as I came in from the garage, I heard that loved voice on the answering machine leaving a message. By the time I got to the phone he had hung up. My prayer had been answered exactly. And I said to the Lord, "Very funny. Next time I'd like to actually speak to him!"

Like any love relationship, ours with the Lord will deepen in direct proportion to the amount of time we devote to getting to know Him. Studying the Bible gives us a rich opportunity to get to know Him more deeply. And so does spending quiet prayer time with Him outside the noisy camp. How it must delight Him when we step out of our busyness and routine and intentionally lay down our To Do list and sit for a few quiet moments with Him. What gifts He brings to those meetings! What glory! And we rejoin our busy lives refreshed and with a renewed perspective.

My husband is on his way out of town tomorrow, and today a friend stopped by with an apple pie as a belated birthday gift for me. So I have the happy prospect of being home alone this week with a homemade apple pie. But even sweeter and more wondrous is this—I will be home alone this week with the Lord Jesus Christ. He will be with me when I wake each morning and He will guard me as I sleep. He will listen to all I need to talk about and He will share His heart with me. And every morning as I start the day I will wake up knowing He has not taken a single bite of my pie. What a friend we have in Jesus!

In His great love,
Laura

Lord Jesus, I praise You as my Savior and I love You as my friend. Thank You for calling me into a love relationship with you. May all that You have planned in me and through me be accomplished, and may it bring You great glory. Lead me onward in our relationship. Amen.

Let us come before him with thanksgiving and
extol him with music and song.

—PSALM 95:2

3 OCTOBER

Dear Friends,

I have wonderfully sore legs today, my calves are aching. A happy reminder of Saturday when I spent a couple of hours prayer walking, (prayer hiking it felt like!) up and down the hills of my son's college campus near Boston. I made my way from one end of the campus to the other and all the way around. From his dorm building to the cafeteria, the gym, past the clinic, the frat houses, the student center, the pizza place where I know he'll be spending a lot of time, his friends' dorm, around to each classroom building and down into the basement of the library—the quietest spot he's found to study. Praying, praying all the way.

My long walk was not just litany of requests but also an extended time of Thanksgiving to God for all he has done and is planning to do in and for and through Peter. I was "preparing the way" for God to show Himself to Peter in every aspect of his college life.

I urge you to take your prayer time on the road. Is your husband struggling at work? Go walk around his place of business praying for him and praising God for all the ways He is at work in your husband's life. Prayer walking around the perimeter of your child's school or preschool is an act of faith and a way to honor God and to acknowledge His power and protection. You can prayer walk around the studio where your granddaughter's dance recital will be. I know a mom who prayer walked around the courthouse where her son was on trial. No one needs to know what you're up to. My son didn't even know I was on campus that Saturday morning as he slept in. You'll look to passersby like a woman out for some sun and exercise, but we know better—Kingdom work!

And as you pray, wherever you pray this week, remember that Praise and Thanksgiving are not mere prefaces to "real" prayers. They are not the seasoning of the skillet or greasing the wheels or charming the host before we get down to the business of asking for things. Praise and Thanks are vital ends in themselves. Praise alone. Thanks alone. Each is complete prayer.

I end with one of the sweetest moments of my Saturday. At one point I was humming the hymn, "Praise to the Lord, the Almighty, the King of Creation . . . " But I had hummed just the first four notes—"Praise to the Lord . . . " when a woman *walking in the opposite direction, picked it up as she passed me on the sidewalk and began to hum the rest of* the line, "The Almighty, the King of Creation . . . " Praise spreads! Pass it on!

Love,

Laura

We praise You, Heavenly Father, as the One who is with our children when we are not. We praise You for this weapon and work and gift You have given us in prayer. Guide us in it, take us deeper. Use us and join us in it. Thank You for Your presence with us and Your power at work in us. We praise Your holy name, Jesus Christ. Amen.

We do not make requests of you because we are righteous,
but because of your great mercy. O Lord, listen! O Lord, forgive!

— DANIEL 9:18

10 OCTOBER

Dear Friends,

I kept busy yesterday. Too busy, because none of the household tasks with which I occupied myself were the things I was supposed to be doing. All day the Lord was calling me to prayer, specifically to confession. And I was pretending not to hear.

I had asked Him in recent days to search me, to point out to me anything I had not recognized as sin. I wanted to clear away any debris that might be polluting or impeding the flow of fresh, clean communication between us, and He had taken me at my word. Now He was calling a meeting and I was afraid to hear what He had come up with. I turned to my big file cabinet that I had decided just had to be cleaned out that day. And after years of neglect the garage seemed to need a lot attention. I wore myself out.

Not surprisingly, I couldn't sleep last night. I lay in bed physically tired but uneasy. I knew that all day I had not been where I was supposed to be. And knowing I had put it off made me even less inclined to go to Him now. I was reluctant to face Him.

I went, though. I went to prayer. I began by praising God, and I relaxed as I remembered whom I was with. Despite my worry, I wasn't slammed with big bad unsuspected news. Rather, recent conversations began to come to mind and a few situations less recent—a series of small, subtle sins I had allowed to pass by unacknowledged, unconfessed. I looked at them now with fresh eyes in the pure light of who He is. I agreed with Him in calling them sin. It was a far-ranging conversation. And when it was through I opened my Bible to a sweet and welcome reminder, Hebrews 2:11: *He purifies people from their sins, and both he and those who are made pure all have the same Father. That is why Jesus is not ashamed to call them his brothers.*

He was not ashamed of me. And He was not granting his forgiveness grudgingly. In fact, once again He was claiming me as His own—dear and close to Him as a sister! Amazing grace. Amazing, every time.

What had I feared? Why had I waited so long? How foolish I had been to delay this relief, this welcome home.

Take time apart with Him today. Be silent and listen, and especially do not fear. Allow Him to speak to you face to face, as a man speaks to a friend. Allow Him to shine His light where needed. He is not standing over us annoyed, hands on hips. His arms are outstretched, calling us in.

In His Great Love,
Laura

Lord, may we respond rightly to Your work in us. May we be quick to come to You in confession. May we be willing to sit with You, to listen, and to respond in one accord with You. Cleanse us; make us more fully Your own. We ask it for Your glory. Amen.

The heart of the wise inclines to the right . . .

—ECCLESIASTES 10:2

17 OCTOBER

Dear Friends,

This morning I read Mark 11:25, which begins with Jesus saying, "And when you stand praying . . ." That caught my eye. As far as I can remember I haven't stood praying lately. It reminded me of how many prayer postures are pictured in the Bible. Jesus "fell with his face to the ground and prayed" (Matthew 26:39). He "knelt down and prayed" (Luke 22:41). In John 17:1 at the dinner table He "looked toward heaven and prayed." Prayers are offered with hands lifted, with heads bowed, sitting, standing, and lying down.

As church began this week, the man in front of me was sitting alone. A few minutes into the service his wife slipped in. It was obvious they belonged together not only because she took the seat beside him but also because she immediately slipped her right hand under his arm. Throughout the service she sat with her whole body and head tilted slightly in his direction. Her adult daughter, sitting on her left, would occasionally lean in to whisper a comment or question and the woman would respond, but by posture and touch she stayed oriented toward and connected to her husband. And at the end of the service, as the congregation rose, she and her husband reached for each others' hands at precisely the same instant. It was a tiny, private gesture and beautiful to see. Without a word exchanged, volumes were spoken between them and about them as a couple.

Those moments that I witnessed of a loving, respectful, long-standing marriage also pictured to me our most important prayer posture as the bride of Christ—holding onto Him and leaning toward right. In our prayer closet, stuck in traffic, wherever we arrive throughout our day He is already there waiting for us. We have only to settle in beside Him and slip our hand into His through prayer. We study the Bible, we incline ourselves toward Him. We lean in to hear His every word, we lean in to whisper our secret pain. And when our time of prayer ends and we rise to head back out into the world, He reaches for our hand at the very instant that we reach for His. We don't even need to look to locate that hand. It is right where we know it will be and is already reaching for ours. We head out there neither alone nor empty-handed.

He doesn't merely tolerate our chatter or good-naturedly pat our reaching hand. He is reaching for our hand even more eagerly than we reach for His. After all, this was entirely His idea—this fellowship, this salvation, this thing called prayer, this new life in Christ. He so wanted the feel of our hand in His that He came to die to make it possible. He reached across the impossible divide to each of us. Kneeling or standing, lean in. Thank Him for saving you a seat.

> Hand in hand with you
> and Him,
> Laura

Father, thank You for all the ways You pictured Your love to us throughout this week. Thank You that You share our desire and our need to be very close in prayer. Help us to remember that amazing truth and to faithfully come to prayer for Your sake as well as for our own. Thank You for putting Mary and Gene right in front of me at church and for illustrating, through their love for each other, Your love for each of us. We love You, too. Amen.

. . . crowds of people came to hear him and
to be healed of their sicknesses.
But Jesus often withdrew to lonely places and prayed

—LUKE 5:15–16

24 OCTOBER

Dear Friends,

I remember when I was asked to pray about joining the leadership of a Community Bible Study class. I said I would pray about it, and I did, but I was sure that leadership was not what God planned for me. I prefer study and prayer at home alone to time in a crowd. I worried about the time commitment too. I wondered if serving in a Bible study class would cost me too much personal prayer and study time.

The Teaching Director was to call me at 11:00 on a Friday and as I waited for her call (prepared to say no to leadership) I was reading *Mere Christianity* by C.S. Lewis. As I read, I came to this line: "you may realize that instead of saying your prayers, you ought to be downstairs writing a letter, or helping your wife to wash-up. Well, go and do it."

Go and do it. Get up out of your chair and go. Serve. What a perfectly timed and needed correction that was for me. If He wanted us to spend all our time meditating on His Word and communing with Him, He would have taken us to heaven the minute we trusted Him as Lord. But He didn't. He left us here for a reason—we are here to serve His purposes on earth. We are here as His hands and feet and the mouths through which He speaks—the body of Christ, indeed.

Study and private prayer are critical to our maturing and strengthening as His, but we are here to serve. Balancing study and service is vital. By nature and personality each of us is more inclined toward one than the other. But we must purposefully spend time in both spheres— service and study. Our vitality and effectiveness in service will be fueled by our time spent with Him in solitude. And our study is most satisfying and fruitful when we need to fill up on Him because He has made good and active use of us in others' lives.

Our service brings us into the needy, noisy world literally dying to hear the Truth that we are so privileged to carry in our hearts. We are equipped by Him to share it in a multitude of ways. It is the greatest privilege there is, and He honors us with the task. And it is one for which we are prepared by prayer and study. It is one through which we ourselves are healed and stretched and blessed.

Keep in mind the incredible image we find in Exodus 33 of all of the Israelites rising to their feet as Moses passed by on his way out of camp to be alone with God. The time we take to be alone with God is worthy of such reverence. And when we return to camp, energized and ready to serve, our faces—like the face of Moses—will glow with having been in the presence of God, and that shine will illuminate every life we are privileged to touch in His service.

with love, in Him,
Laura

Almighty God, thank You for Your twin gifts of study and service. Because You created each of us with a particular temperament one of the two is going to be more comfortable than the other. Help each of us with the one that is more of a personal challenge. We trust that we can be most useful to You and most blessed ourselves when they are paired in our lives. Help that to be so. Thank You for hearing us. We ask this for Your glory. Amen.

Then those who feared the Lord talked with each other, and
the Lord listened and heard. A scroll of remembrance was written
in his presence concerning those who feared the Lord and honored
his name. "They will be mine," says the Lord Almighty,
"in the day when I make up my treasured possession."

—MALACHI 3:16-17

31 OCTOBER

Dear Friends,

We often talk about prayer and what it means to us and offers to us, but have you ever considered prayer from God's perspective? I heard a friend this week beautifully compare her longing to hear her late mother's voice with God longing to hear from His children in prayer. "God is waiting for your call, to hear your voice say, 'I am thinking of You today.'"

I was delighted by a call from my son at college last week. He was full of news. "Pete called today!" I happily reported to my husband that evening.

"I know. I told him to."

My heart sank. What a loss. Same good visit, same sharing and laughing and information relayed. But the sharing was diminished somehow when I learned it was perhaps initiated not by Pete but at someone else's instigation.

We are loved by God with a Father's love, and our prayers bring Him joy. But He wants us near and sharing our lives and hearts with Him not out of obligation but in love, choosing to share our hearts and lives with Him. And He makes astounding promises to those desiring to be near to Him and to know Him.

One of my favorite promises in all Scripture is Psalm 25:14: *The LORD confides in those who fear him; he makes his covenant known to them.* We share our secrets with those closest to us and the Lord promises to do the same. Don't you want to be one of those who are in the Lord's inner circle as Peter and John and James were? Those few who spent the most time with Him saw the greatest miracles— things like the Transfiguration, things others were not permitted to see.

Incredibly, as we share our hearts with God in prayer He promises to share His heart with us as well. *Call to me and I will answer you and tell you great and unsearchable things you do not know.* (Jeremiah 33:3)

Prayer can be a desperate call sent out to a faceless, efficient emergency dispatcher or it can be our call home to a loving Father who is as near as a whisper. It can be a dry act of obedience or it can be the gateway to blessing, to confidences shared, to great and unsearchable things we cannot imagine.

With You in Him,
Laura

Lord God, as this new week begins, draw near to us as we, with expectant hearts, draw near to You. Purify our communion with You, our love for You, our desire to know You and spend our lives in Your presence. Show us what You will. Open our eyes, open our hearts to You. For Your glory. Amen.

The Lord is not slow in keeping his promise,
as some understand slowness.
He is patient with you, not wanting anyone to perish,
but everyone to come to repentance.

— 2 PETER 3:9

7 NOVEMBER

Dear Friends,

My friend Cindy told a beautiful story this week demonstrating God's power to bring one man to faith, a seemingly "hopeless case." God used the prayers of faithful friends like Cindy and her group of praying friends. Did you know that God uses the prayers of believers to draw unbelievers to Himself? We are used as John the Baptist was used to "prepare the way of the Lord." Prayers prepare the seedbed—the hearts of our loved ones—to accept Christ's forgiveness.

God said to a man in Job 42:7-8, *"I am angry with you . . . because you have not spoken of me what is right, as my servant Job has . . . My servant Job will pray for you, and I will accept his prayer and not deal with you according to your folly."* What a promise! The Lord will accept our prayers on behalf of our friends. What a relief and privilege and assignment. Our loved ones may not be praying to the Lord, but God promises to hear our prayers on their behalf. How lovingly the Lord provides for us, even in our unbelief.

There is a passage in Luke 5 that says that the sins of the paralytic were forgiven when Jesus saw the faith of the man's *friends.* They, filled with faith, had carried him on his mat to Jesus. How do we carry our loved ones to Christ? By prayer. That is our loving labor—carrying them to Him and laying them at His feet.

And not giving up. Cindy and her friends prayed for their friend's salvation not for weeks. Not for months. It was years. Pray believing, and do not get discouraged if you don't see results as fast as you want them. His timing is perfect. Your part is to pray, His part is to save.

Do you know who prayed for you to come to faith? Someone did. Maybe many did. You may not learn who all of them were until you get to heaven. Last year I found an old letter written to me by my brother Nick in 1981, seven years before I came to faith. It's a letter I don't remember receiving. It told me he was praying for my salvation. I learned recently that my great-grandmother Mattye, whom I never knew, was a deeply committed Christian and a woman of prayer. I have no doubt that she prayed faithfully for my mother and her not-yet-born children. Are you praying for the salvation of your great-grandchildren who won't be born until 2040?

Praise Him for what He is planning in answer to your prayers. Thank Him for all those who prayed for you to come to faith, the ones you know about and the ones you don't. Pray others in. This is one neighborhood we want to see exploding with growth!

With you in Him,
Laura

Our Father, Thank you for this gift of prayer. Please lay on my heart those whom You would have me pray for until they are safely Yours. And may I faithfully do so. Increase my dedication to prayer and my understanding of it and of how You use prayer to accomplish Your purposes on this earth. We claim the promise of Your word that says You desire all men to be saved. Use me as You will. Amen.

Acknowledge and take to heart this day that the LORD is
God in heaven above and on the earth below. There is no other.

— DEUTERONOMY 4:39

14 NOVEMBER

Dear Friends,

Three years ago my young friend Meg was dying of cancer. I spent
a lot of time with her because she had no family in the area and
wanted to stay in California as long as she could. Her neighbor
Ellen and I took care of almost everything. We took her to chemo
and radiation, we took comprehensive notes during heart-breaking
doctor visits, we grocery shopped and arranged meals and oversaw
an extensive prayer chain. We did errands and filled prescriptions
and sat with her. Whenever she closed her eyes a moment, I gratefully studied that loved face. We prayed and loved her and thanked
God for every bit of time we had with her.

Nevertheless, the one Meg most wanted to be with was Carl the
no-good boyfriend. They had met a few months earlier and he had
broken up with her after the cancer had spread to her brain. This
was the person she kept phoning and reaching for and talking about
to us during our precious, diminishing time together. It was maddening! I had known and loved Meg for eleven years and was giving her huge amounts of my time and energy, grateful for every
minute I was granted with her. I was almost desperately counting
down the time I had left with my beloved friend. And yet whenever
I appeared, it felt as if she was looking past me in search of the one
she really wanted. One day, as I angrily scribbled all this in my
prayer journal, and ranted about the unfairness of it and the pain,
the Lord seemed to say to me quietly, shockingly: "Now you know
how I feel."

The One who most loves me has literally given His life for me.
Jesus Christ, unending source of all I have and need, is the One to

whom I have instant and continual access. And yet I look past Him for something better. I bypass prayer and pick up the phone. Or the remote. Or the fork. I turn to all my false, familiar sources of comfort and distraction.

Christ Himself fashioned every one of the needs I have. And He did so for the sole purpose of lovingly meeting each one. Every longing of my heart represents an opportunity for Him to display His perfect, sufficient provision. And He has promised He will do just that if I will only turn to Him instead of the pale, pathetic substitutes I tend to prefer.

Love the Lord your God with all your heart, He said to me this weekend. He knows that my heart is not wholly His. I am often unfaithful. My affection is divided and, in some directions, is completely misplaced and wasted.

I am learning to be true: Christ is the One who loves me. Prayer is the continual conversation with that Friend who so loves the sight of my face that He never looks away. He happily anticipates our every talk; He savors every minute we have together, never mindful of the clock—He knows we have eternity.

With you in Him,
Laura

Lord God, Thank You that there is no such thing as unrequited love in the life of a believer, only misplaced affection. I am sorry for all the unholy things I have expected You to share my crowded heart space with. Teach me to love You with all of my heart. I ask this for Your honor. Amen.

. . . this happened so that the work of
God might be displayed in his life.

—JOHN 9:3

21 NOVEMBER

Dear Friends,

Thanksgiving is here so suddenly and kicks off what will surely be a full, fast six or seven weeks until, God willing, we will find ourselves in a new year.

This seems to be the natural time of year to enumerate all the things in our lives for which we are thankful. Particularly after a year like this last one during which natural disasters and wars and disease have been so much in the news and on our hearts. We are quick to thank the Lord for our warm, dry houses, for our health and loving family members.

But God is Lord of all. As surely as He sent the beautiful weather we enjoy and provided the homes to which we retreat each evening, He also sent that tiresome relative who's heading to your house for Thanksgiving dinner. God is also behind the phone call that came in saying your daughter isn't coming home this week after all. God knows about the challenges resulting from your mom's stroke last spring and what her absence in the kitchen and at the table this Thursday will mean to you. We think these are things that slipped past God when He was making His plans for our week. But in fact they passed in full view of His throne just like everything else that is in the works.

What is the most challenging thing you face this week? What do you most dread about the upcoming holiday? What is the one thing you would choose to remove from the plan, the thing without which you think this would be a perfect holiday? Think about that person or circumstance or prospect. That is exactly where God is at work in your heart, in your life. It is where He is focusing

His attention in His on-going improvement project of making you more Christlike. And as such, that tender spot in your life—whatever it may be—is holy ground, for God is at work there. We must tread very carefully in these areas of our lives. These are the places where we are, perhaps, not fully yielded to God. These are the areas where we must guard our words and actions and attitudes with particular care.

It is exciting to look at these old things with new eyes. To lay aside our usual perspective, our human, tired, fed-up way of looking at this situation and to choose to look at it spiritually. How might God be at work in this? What might He chiseling away in me?

Take to Him in prayer this week all those areas over which you think even He can't prevail. He is already there and hard at work. He is only waiting for us to catch up and to join Him in what He is doing. Let this be the year we look in a new way at what may be years-old challenges. Forget what that annoying relative is doing. What is God doing? That's what matters. It is something for your good and for His glory. It is something loving and righteous.

We think we have to live our Christian lives despite this and that. But we have been promised that it is exactly in these challenges that the victory of Christ will most gloriously be displayed in our lives.

Thankful for you,
Laura

Heavenly Father, Thank You for all You have given and are doing. Open my eyes to what You are working out of me through these challenges and thorns and pain. Help me hand over to You the thing I most deeply want to be free of. Thank You. Thank You! In Jesus' name. Amen.

Yet I am always with you; you hold me by my right hand.
You guide me with your counsel and afterward you will take me
into glory. Whom have I have in heaven but you?
And earth has nothing I desire besides you.

— PSALM 73:23-25

28 NOVEMBER

Dear Friends,

For ten years I had a very satisfying relationship with my cat. He greeted me at the door when I came home (he knows the sound of my car). He came and lay on my lap whenever I sat down. Throughout the day he tended to be in the same room as I was simply because he liked my company. But things are different now.

Two weeks ago I gave him a treat—a small chewy thing that looks like a wine cork. The vet said it takes a while to chew up and in the process the cat's teeth will be cleaned. Well, nice theory but it doesn't work out that way. This cat doesn't chew the thing; he likes the taste so much that he wolfs it down in two big bites. And the instant his mouth is empty he starts yowling for more. I have had to put the bag in the top drawer of a six-foot-tall dresser so he can't reach it.

A cat that used to have a fairly wide-ranging (and quiet) existence spends much of his time now hanging around the dresser gazing upward in expectation and yowling for all he's worth. He no longer sits peacefully on my lap. He no longer takes any notice of me at all except to track my proximity to the dresser. When putting away clean clothes, I have to tip-toe upstairs and try to sneak open the sock drawer before a 9-pound furry rocket blasts toward me at the first squeak of the dresser drawer. In short, feline fellowship has been broken.

In the same way, enjoyment of God's blessings can so easily slide into something else, something that to Him must be loss. Our focus shifts from Giver to gift to self. I want to approach the Lord in prayer without looking to see what's in His hand. I want my praise and my faithfulness to be completely divorced from what I do or don't get from Him.

Our aim as believers is increasingly to know and to glorify Him. That's why part of our prayer time is dedicated to praising Him for who He is. We praise Him for all those qualities and names by which He is known. We need make no reference to ourselves or our lives at all. This is His time. One method of praise is simply to say, "Almighty God, You are ___" and fill in the blank with any of His names and qualities. Take your time to consider each one. "Father, You are Holy. You are Sovereign. Omnipotent. Unchanging. You are the good shepherd. You are Counselor. You are Wise. Eternal. Savior."

Dedicate some this week to prayer that is focused entirely on who God is—not asking for anything, not thanking Him for anything. It will come haltingly at first, but keep at it. As praise becomes more natural to us, we make great leaps in our understanding of who God is. And that leads inevitably to greater faith and greater praise and greater glory to God.

Love,
Laura

Almighty God, May we look heavenward throughout this week not yowling for more but silent and awestruck. May You be glorified by the attitudes of our hearts as we come to You in prayer. Hallowed be Your Name. Amen.

Sing to the LORD a new song, for he has done marvelous things;
his right hand and his holy arm have worked salvation for him.

—PSALM 98:1

5 DECEMBER

Dear Friends,

When I was in high school, I had the same First Period class every single day all four years—Chorus with Mr. Dunn. I loved the beauty and power of 200 voices singing together in four-part harmony. We sang incredible music, much of it sacred.

Our home life was challenging during those years and stepping into that music room each morning was a blessed, calming gift. And that was due largely to Mr. Dunn himself—a caring man and great teacher who was passionate about music and the most graceful of conductors. Watching him work was like watching a ballet. He was transported by the music and would cry out to us, "Listen to what you're saying! Listen to the words!"

The words! They have been in my heart ever since: "Blessed are they that mourn, for they shall be comforted." "As one whom his own mother comforts, I will comfort you." "Ye know that for a little time labor and sorrow were mine, but at the last, I have found comfort." "How lovely is Thy dwelling place, Oh Lord of Hosts." Years before I came to true faith, the Lord had me reciting God's Word each morning and filling up on His promises.

Fast forward fifteen years. My father had just died and I headed back east to the funeral. My dad, also a music lover, had been a member of a community chorus and that group attended his funeral to perform "Jesu, Joy of Man's Desiring." As they lined up to sing, I sat in the congregation weeping and trying to prepare myself for the eulogy I had composed and was about to give. I couldn't imagine how I was going to speak publicly in such a broken state. I kept whispering to my husband that I couldn't do it. And then the music began and I watched none other than Mr. Dunn step up to conduct the chorus.

The Lord could not have chosen anyone from all my life doing anything more moving to me or fortifying than the sight of Mr. Dunn conducting that magnificent music. His fluid arm movements and those lovely, eloquent hand gestures soothed me as they always had many years before. In the moment when I most needed it the Lord orchestrated for me the most comforting image possible. And minutes later it allowed me to stand up and do one of the hardest things I had ever done.

As you pray this week, thank God for the people He has used throughout your life to comfort and instruct you and even, perhaps unknowingly, to point you to Him.

In Christ,
Laura

Blessed Lord! We raise our voices in prayer to sing to You a song of praise. We marvel at Your work in our lives. Long before we had the sense to look to You, Your eyes were upon us in love, and You were planning our redemption. We praise Your name! Amen.

I will bless you . . . and you will be a blessing.

—GENESIS 12:2

12 DECEMBER

Dear Friends,

One day last week I had the most wonderful taste of God's goodness. The Christmas cookies from a cookie exchange I'd had with friends sat on my kitchen counter. I was still undecided about whom to give them to. I could give them to a neighbor, but which one? I didn't want to play favorites. I knew my husband and I wouldn't (and shouldn't) eat them all, so I suggested he take them to the office. But his small office is so well stocked with treats this time of year I decided to give them to a neighbor after all, and somewhat arbitrarily chose one. I wrote out a gift tag, stuck it on the plastic lid, and headed for the door. On my way out I grabbed two letters that needed to be mailed.

As I stepped out of the house I saw our mail carrier one house away. "Perfect timing!" I called to her. When tired, overworked Alma looked up and saw me with cookies in my hand, a huge smile of gratitude broke over her face.

"Oh, Laura!" she said, "I can't believe it! I'll be right there." I surreptitiously peeled off the gift tag as she pulled up to our mailbox.

"That is the nicest thing I have ever seen! Homemade cookies! This will be perfect with my thermos of coffee. Did you make all these?"

I told her that I and a lot of friends had made them. "I can't believe this!" she said again.

"God bless you" I told her. "God bless you too!" she said, hugging me.

Over the years I have thought of all sorts of creative ways to talk to this lady about God's love, but in one surprising moment the

Lord poured His love all over her in a sweet, tangible way. I had nothing at all to do with it and yet I received a gift too—the joy of being delivery girl.

The entire delightful exchange was a grand reminder that *"every good and perfect gift is from above, coming down from the Father* (James 1:17). God's plan is so much greater than ours; it is perfect. And only He knows the deepest needs of each heart. If in prayer we will only yield to Him our plans for today and our schedule and our God-given talents and our willingness to be used, He will take all of it and redirect it and magnify it and create masterpieces of perfect timing and perfect love.

We may not know until heaven how He has used us. The cookies I and my friends made last week when we had no time to make them greatly blessed an exhausted mail carrier named Alma. God willing, we will share the joy in heaven of seeing her and countless others approach us with grateful smiles.

Amazingly enough, you and I are the means through which the Lord has chosen to express His love to this dying world. What fun! What a gift to us! As you open your eyes each morning, let your first waking thought be a prayer—"Make me a blessing today, Lord."

Love,
Laura

Almighty God, Thank You for that incomparable sense of joy when I know I am exactly where You want me to be and am doing exactly what You want me to be doing. Guide me, lead me, so that more and more I know that solid sense of relief and rightness in being about Your business. In Christ's holy name, Amen.

To him who sits on the throne and to the Lamb be praise
and honor and power for ever and ever!

— REVELATION 5:13

19 DECEMBER

Dear Friends,

Talking to my brother Toby yesterday, who is housebound in icy North Carolina, we laughingly remembered one of the greatest joys of our childhood in suburban New York. On winter mornings very often it was the sound of snowplows that woke us early on school days. I would hop out of bed at the sound and race to my bedroom window hoping to see some serious weather. Then it was down to the chilly kitchen with my brothers to huddle around the radio tuned to WVIP, the local station.

Squirming, elbowing each other, chewing on knuckles, praying what were likely the most fervent prayers of our childhood, we waited and hoped and listened for the words we most wanted to hear. And then they would come: "Due to inclement weather, Chappaqua District schools will be closed today."

YAY! Screams of victory and joy, cats and dogs scattering in alarm, prayer time past in an instant, racing minds beginning to anticipate all the fun ahead: Sledding instead geography, baking instead of science, afternoon TV instead of math. A fire in the fireplace. Lying in with cocoa and favorite books and Carrie, Esmè, Morgan & Topaz —all the dogs and cats who had reconvened to revel in the presence of so many warm bodies sprawled all over the house.

On an ordinary day, in the dark, in the cold, unanticipated blessing came to us. It was a blessing we had no power to make happen for ourselves but one that brought with it comfort and joy and fun and all the pleasures of a warm home with a well-stocked pantry and a large fireplace. I'm quite sure I never took the time to thank

God for those grand days, so I did so today. And it occurs to me that snow days were one childhood joy my own son, growing up in San Diego, never knew.

But he does know the unanticipated, unearned joy of a greater gift—the birth of Jesus. The coming to earth of God Almighty to live among us and suffer alongside us and earn for us, through His willing death, complete forgiveness and an eternal home with Him. It won't be snow plows that signals the joy of His return but the sound of a trumpet.

Remember this week what we are celebrating. Remember to Thank Him Thank Him Thank Him for the words we most wanted to hear all our lives, even before we knew enough to hope for them: *Fear not, for I have redeemed you; I have summoned you by name; you are mine. When you pass through the waters I will be with you; and when you pass through the rivers, they will not sweep over you. . . . For I am the LORD, your God, the Holy One of Israel, your Savior . . . I, even I am he who blots out your transgressions, for my own sake, and remembers your sin no more.*

May God bless you this Christmas week with a new appreciation of who He is,

Laura

Almighty God, Thank you. For coming in human form as Jesus, for living among us, for dying to redeem us, for indwelling us as Comforter and Counselor, for preparing for us an eternal home in Your presence. We thank You as our Redeemer. We praise You as our King. Amen.

To God's elect, strangers in the world . . .

— 1 PETER 1:1

26 DECEMBER

Dear Friends,

Our son, Peter, returned home from college the other night. What a happy reunion! He has been away from home longer than ever before and is so glad to be back where everything is familiar and welcoming. He walked through the house that first night looking at everything with renewed appreciation and affection.

We were as happy to see his too-long hair as the smile underneath it, his over-full dirty clothes bag as the bag full of Christmas gifts. He and everything he brought with him were embraced—the tales of successes and of failures, the recounting of good experiences and the upsetting ones. We were grateful to be sharing in all of it.

And it made me think about what it must have been like when Jesus returned home after 33 years away. Imagine the joy in heaven, the celebration! I can just see the angels gathered on the banks of the River of Life shaking out His big bag of laundry.

"I'm so glad He's home!"

"Me too. It just hasn't been the same without Him."

"Time flies! It's been years, and yet it almost seems like just a moment."

"And doesn't He look good?"

"Wonderful!"

"You can tell He's happy to be home. His face just glows!"

"Hand me the bleach."

"You know, I don't think we're going to need it. This stuff looks pretty clean."

"You're right! My goodness, it looks white as snow."

Heaven! Peter (the saint in the Bible not the one in my house) reminds us that this world is not our home. As familiar and comfortable and love-filled as our homes may be here, we have so much more to look forward to in heaven. Last year when my brother Nick first learned he had cancer, he said to me of heaven, "Laura! We are going to see colors we have never seen! We are going to hear music we have never heard!" We are going to hear words of welcome and love we have never imagined. We are going to have a sense of belonging and acceptance we have never known.

Live your lives as strangers here with reverent fear. For you know that it was not with perishable things such as silver and gold that you were redeemed from the empty way of life handed down to you from your forefathers, but with the precious blood of Christ . . . (1 Peter 1:17-18)

Even as we celebrate His birth, thank Him for His death—the purpose of His appearing. Thank Him for His redemption, which opened for us the gates of heaven.

He has gone before us into the new year as surely as He has gone before and awaits our eventual homecoming. Recommit yourself to Him in prayer—your time and your hurts and your desires and your talents, for as long as He has you here.

With you in Him,
Laura

Thank you, Father, for stooping down to redeem us, for making a way for us to come to You. May we remember that our time is not our own; we are here on your errand. Use us how You will for Your glory, and keep our eyes on You. In Christ's name. Amen.

Therefore if anyone is in Christ, he is a new creation;
the old has gone, the new has come!
All this is from God, who reconciled us
to himself through Christ.

— 2 CORINTHIANS 5:17-18

2 JANUARY

Dear Friends,

One day last week I had ice cream and cookies for dinner. Doesn't that sound like fun? But the fact is, I only had such a meal because the hospital cafeteria was locking up for the night as I came looking for dinner. I was only allowed through the door because I'd agreed to grab what was handy, and to hurry through the check-out line. So ice cream and cookies it was. "This would be fun under other circumstances," I thought.

I had been at my brother Nick's bedside all week in the adult oncology unit. He'd had a stroke on Friday, Christmas was Sunday, and the leukemia diagnosis came on Monday. Often through the week I've thought of how grim this vigil should be, but oddly enough we're actually having a wonderful visit. We're getting to know each other as adults and liking what we find. We're getting to know each other as believers and celebrating what we share. We're laughing a lot. I'm discovering that Nick has an incredible sense of humor; it's wonderfully reminiscent of the great wit of our father, gone almost twenty years. We're ending the long days in prayer. We're praying for our younger brother, Toby, far away and worried. "This would be unbearable under other circumstances," I thought.

I woke this morning thanking God for the time together. I am ending the day praising God for His mercies, for redemption, for restoring to us the years the locusts had eaten.

Nick and Toby and I shared a childhood we rarely make reference to. We spent our adult years out of touch with each other because avoidance was easier than the painful memories that tended to haunt phone calls or visits. The simplest exchanges brought with them so much that was unbidden and unwelcome, so we traded it all for silence.

Family loyalty came roaring back, though, eighteen months ago when Nick called for the first time in ten years to say he'd been diagnosed with lymphoma. "I need you," (unspoken but understood) and the old life was gone in a blink.

When we come to Christ at long last, recognizing our need for what He alone can give, our prayerful "I need you" is met instantly with new life. And our transformed lives become the means through which He spreads the Word. *We are therefore Christ's ambassadors, as though God were making his appeal through us. We implore you on Christ's behalf: be reconciled to God.* (2 Corinthians 5:20).

Thank God today for your forgiveness, for new life in Christ. Faithfully pray for unbelieving family members. Years before I came to faith, Nick was praying for me. He knew my true need long before I did. I will enjoy eternal blessings because of Nick's faithfulness as Christ's ambassador. Pray! Pray! Pray!

> With you in Christ,
> Laura

Holy Spirit of God, pour into my loved one. Make yourself known to him who does not yet know You but is so hungry for truth. Draw him with loving kindness, redeem him for Your glory. Use me however You will to make Yourself known. In Christ's name, Amen.

As for me, far be it from me that I should sin
against the LORD by failing to pray for you.

— 1 SAMUEL 12:23

9 JANUARY

Dear Friends,

We are off to an intense start of this new year with a lot of difficult news coming to us of loved ones. It has been easy to feel overwhelmed or hopeless or helpless. Yesterday I felt particularly anxious to DO something. I jumped into the car first thing in the morning and headed out into activity, errands, good deeds, practical tasks. Along the way I phoned friends in search of answers or comfort. None of it satisfied, of course. And worse, none of it served my suffering loved ones.

I ended up where I should have begun—in quiet, in prayer, surrendering once more, admitting my uselessness and my helplessness under what seem to be such daunting circumstances. I ended up, in short, exactly where God wants me.

When Shadrach, Meshach and Abednego were thrown into the fiery furnace by Nebuchadnezzar, perhaps they had friends standing at some distance from that furnace watching them being thrown in. Perhaps Daniel was there. He was their close friend. How might he have responded? Do you think Daniel said the very foolish thing we say when we feel helpless? "Well, all we can do is pray . . ."

Ludicrous thought! Daniel was a man who *lived* to serve God. He knew and loved his God, our God. Never would he have responded by slowly, mournfully shaking his head. Daniel certainly prayed for his friends, but with passion! In full voice! With head up and in full assurance of being heard. He prayed with confidence to the God he *knew* was able to save his friends, the God he *knew* heard his prayers and was willing to act upon them.

The greatest thing each one of us can do for our loved ones is to get to know our sovereign God, to deepen our relationship with Him. Our prayers, rooted in our certainty of God's power and His unfailing love, will make us priceless friends and mothers and wives and sisters. Women of the greatest power in this world. *Never* would we say, "all we can do is pray." *Never* would prayer be our last resort but *always* our first response. And our greatest strength.

We have lost our confidence in prayer. We have lost our reverence for prayer. And it happened when we began to trust in ourselves and our own efforts. My loved ones in desperate trouble have no need for my meager human offerings. They need the power and provision of Almighty God. And on their behalf I have it in my power to engage His loving hand. We have been given the keys to the kingdom! And we need to learn how to use them. We need to get to know the God whom we serve and we need to trust in this holy gift called prayer. Never belittle it or insult our God by repeating those seven words with a hopeless air. Prayer is the greatest gift we can give!

With you in Him,
Laura

Almighty God, have mercy on our loved ones. Keep our eyes and their eyes on You, and forgive us our doubt. May every one of Your holy purposes be accomplished in these circumstances. May You be glorified in them and through them. Use us how You will. We are Your servants. We come to You with full assurance of being heard, through Christ, our Lord. Amen.

You have forgotten God your Savior;
you have not remembered the Rock, your fortress.

—ISAIAH 17:10

16 JANUARY

Dear Friends,

Almost two years ago I was at the San Diego airport early one morning and I was not a happy camper. I was there with my husband and son, and we were on our way to look at colleges. We were going to be in five states in nine days looking at eleven schools.

This was not the first step in the college search process, but for me this was the one that made it real. Peter was truly going to leave home. And he was going to be truly far away—all the schools he was considering were on the east coast.

I was dreading the trip itself—multiple flights, almost every night in a different hotel, a packed schedule with a 3-hour time change, but most of all, overarching everything else was that pervading sense that loss was looming not very far in our future when Peter would walk out the door.

So you have the picture as I stepped up to the US Airways counter and handed the agent our tickets. And the agent, his name was Al C., flipped through the many pages of our complicated itinerary and he looked up at Peter and then looked over me and gave me a huge grin and he said, "Well, *this* looks like the start of a great adventure!"

And with that, everything changed. My whole perspective was corrected. Because, of course he was absolutely right. This *was* the start of a great adventure. A great chapter in our son's life, a great chapter in our marriage. A great accomplishment. A fun family vacation ahead of us. With one line and a great smile, Al C. completely shifted my focus and ignited my excitement about what was ahead.

I have been working and reworking material for two months to prepare to speak at a women's retreat this weekend. Writing a lot and worrying far too much. And yesterday at church with one line and a smile, a dear friend refocused me, "It is an incredible privilege."

This life we're living with Christ is one of great privilege. We are in the earliest moments of an eternal, rich, great adventure! Don't let the enemy discourage you or divert you from the Truth we know and have experienced over and over: Christ is sovereign. He is unfailingly loving. We can trust Him. That's what we learn during times of calm as we study His Word and spend time in relaxed prayer getting to know Him more deeply. In times of peace we fill up on His Truth so that in times of challenge we have reserves to draw from and fruit to feed upon.

But we are not limited to dried, preserved fruit. We do not have to look *back* to assure ourselves of God's goodness and faithfulness. There is fresh fruit continuously available to us through prayer and His Word. Reach for Him today in prayer. Whether you are in a period of great joy or anticipating loss. Look up! The Lord is still on His throne, high and exalted, and the train of His robe fills the temple.

With you in Him,
Laura

Our Lord and our God, We praise You as Almighty. We acknowledge You as the One who is ruling in all things. May You be glorified in this new week, in this new year. Help us to make You known to those around us by our calm, trusting response to challenges. Amen.

"As soon as you began to pray, an answer was given . . ."

— DANIEL 9:23

23 JANUARY

Dear Friends,

When we involve ourselves in Bible study, and talking and thinking about God and things of God, more and more do we recognize prayer as our best response, whatever the situation. But sometimes I think I settle for the simple relief I find in the act of praying itself. Do we unburden ourselves in prayer thinking of it the way we think of venting to a friend, a friend who can't actually do anything about our aggravation? With a sympathetic human ear we console ourselves with the thought, "Well, at least I'm heard, at least I know I'm not alone in this."

But we have so much more to hope for, of course. The Holy Spirit of God is *in* us and *with* us, as near as our own heartbeat. God is our refuge and strength, an *ever-present* help in trouble. (Psalm 46:1). Ever-present. Always present. Right here, right now. Regardless of circumstances look or whatever our discouragement is telling us.

The reality of prayer is almost beyond our imagining. Our Almighty, unfailingly loving God hears and shares each of our heart concerns. And He *instantly* responds, regardless of whether or not the answer is immediately apparent in human terms. Back in Luke 1, an angel assured Zechariah, (who'd been hoping for *years* for a child), "Your prayer has been heard." In Genesis 16 the angel of the Lord amazed Hagar with the news, "God has heard of your misery." She was amazed because based on her human circumstances— a runaway, alone and pregnant in a desert—there was no reason to believe God knew or cared. But He was present with her. He appeared and spoke to her in that lonely place. And He made great promises about her future and the future of her child. Over and over the Bible assures us that the Lord not only hears but takes joy in responding to believing prayer.

Daniel contains one of the most thrilling promises regarding prayer in all the Bible. In Chapter 9, while Daniel is praying, *"confessing my sin and the sin of my people Israel and making my request to the LORD my God for his holy hill—while I was still in prayer,*

Gabriel . . . came to me." The angel said to Daniel, *"As soon as you began to pray, an answer was given."* What a promise!

God doesn't need to wait for the end of the prayer. We don't pray in order to fill Him in on the situation. We don't pray to bring Him up to speed on the details. He already knows it all. He is watching for that bowed head and prayerful heart. At those signs of our submission, of our trust in Him, our prayer is heard, and an answer is given.

We sometimes forget or do not dare hope: God hears our prayers. He answers prayers. Don't settle for unburdening yourself; pray very specifically. Ask with assurance and confidence. And pray believing.

> With you in Him,
> Laura

Father, You who formed my heart shares every one of my concerns. Help me to pray with greater trust in Your presence and power available to me and Your love for me. Thank You for who You are despite who I am. In Christ's name, Amen

This is what the LORD says, "Stand at the crossroads and look;
ask for the ancient paths, ask where the good way is, and
walk in it, and you will find rest for your souls."

— JEREMIAH 6:16

30 JANUARY

Dear Friends,

Is the thorn in your side a person? Is there someone in your life who knows how to push every button you have and seems to do so with relish? Could your friends recite by heart the litany of annoyances this person has inflicted upon you over the years?

When I recently faced a meeting with one of my thorns, I was given just the counsel and advice I needed by a wise old man of nineteen. He said he'd tell me the same thing he'd told a friend who was struggling with a freshman roommate headache: "*You* do the right thing. Just do what you know you're supposed to do and disregard their reaction. Let them have their fit. Don't get caught up in their nonsense. You have to answer to God alone. Live for an audience of One."

No one serving as a soldier gets involved in civilian affairs—he wants to please his commanding officer. (2 Timothy 2:4) We are here to serve and please God alone. And our promotion exams come disguised as glaring teens and irritating relatives and impossible-to-please bosses.

On a recent trip, as my husband and I waited to take off, the dark clouds that hung over the runway looked threatening. Once we rose above them, though, those same clouds became a part of the larger beautiful landscape we looked down upon. We need to lift our sights beyond the earthly realm. There is so much more going on than we realize—even in our disagreements and conflicts with loved ones. Each is an opportunity to reflect Christ, not self. Each is an opportunity to honor Christ by reacting in a new way. Each is another chance to get it right, to choose the good way.

One thing that each is not, however, is our Last Chance. When we fail, God's love for us is unchanged and we get to try again. His mercy is new every morning. We are given yet another opportunity to respond rightly, to do it better, to see it His way.

My meeting with my thorn went OK, not great. Despite all my good intentions and resolutions, still I found myself responding in the same old defensive, intimidated, nervous manner. But God whispers to me, "I love you. My love for you is unchanged. I won't love you more when you get it right. I don't love you less when you don't."

And, as always when I feel like I've failed a test or mishandled an opportunity to represent Christ, I need to confess it and let it go and not allow it to become an occasion for self-focus or self-condemnation, both of which take my eyes off Him and keep me down and rob me of hope. It is the Holy Spirit who empowers us to live holy lives. *Sanctified* means set apart for holy use, and our sanctification is a life-long process. Join me in praising Him as the God of unfailing love. Join me in praising Him as the Lord who sanctifies.

> With you in Him,
> Laura

Thank You, Father, that You love me right now as perfectly and completely as You always will. Whatever I do You will never love me less. Thank You that Your favor and love are not based on my performance or credentials or looks or poise. And thank You that Your favor and Your love are not held for me until I get to heaven but are mine to rest in even now. Help me to do so, and to live in a way that honors You and points to You, not me. For the honor of Your name and for Your glory, Amen.

"My son," the father said, "you are always with me,
and everything I have is yours."

LUKE 15:31

6 FEBRUARY

Dear Friends,

Do you ever think about your prayers and how they get where
they're going? Where do you imagine they go? Is it enough to simply let them fly and trust that the winds or the angels will get them
wherever they're bound? Do a little imagination game. Close your
eyes and think about a simple prayer and picture its trip. Do you
imagine it rising through the ceiling and roof and on up into the
sky? Through the clouds? Then what? Where do you imagine God
is? Do you imagine a long trip through a big galaxy for that little
prayer? Should we worry that a few may get lost or dropped along
the way? I once had a large deposit of several checks get lost somewhere between the ATM, which acknowledged my deposit, and the
bank, five feet away, which never received any of it. How long
should we expect the trip to take? Is it a safe one? Is it a well-
guarded path? There's an old Jewish expression of agreement and
hope—"From your lips to God's ear." How much of a journey are
we talking about?

No trip at all, of course. Christ is in us. Our prayers are delivered
and already on His heart even as we are putting words to them. The
Bible promises that before we have even finished praying, God already is answering. (Daniel 9:23). We may not see the result with
our human eyes for some time, we may not even live to see it, but
our prayers are immediately heard and treasured and responded to.

We need to trust in *where*—the Lord is—as near as our own
heartbeat—and we need to trust in *who* the Lord is—Almighty
God, who desires even more than we do those things that will glorify and honor Him and will bring about His kingdom. He does not

grant our God-honoring requests grudgingly or with reluctance. Remember the father of the prodigal son—once his son had turned toward home, though still a far way off, his father already was running out to meet him. As soon as our hearts are turned to God in prayer, seeking those things that He also wants, He is *running* to meet those needs.

As I drove along a New York highway in December I was thinking about a loved one's need for hope and peace of mind. I was weighing various ways I could get the Word of God into his hands and heart. But I realized then with a laugh that the Lord knows his needs far better than I do and He knows how best to meet them. With that realization I turned from plotting to prayer. I asked God Himself to provide for my loved one. Before I had even finished the brief prayer I drove past the most unlikely and thrilling sight. Someone had erected a large hand-painted sign in the snowy woods alongside the road. It shouted in fat black letters: "God Answers Prayer!"

with you in Him,
Laura

Father, Help me to remember that Your ways are not my ways and to trust in Your unfailing love. May Your life in me increasingly prevail against my human will. May I live with ever-increasing abandon to You. May my prayers more and more reflect Your divine will, that Your kingdom may come on earth as it is in heaven. For Your glory, Amen.

For our light and momentary troubles are achieving for us an
eternal glory that far outweighs them all. So we fix our eyes not
on what is seen, but on what is unseen. For what is seen
in temporary, but what is unseen in eternal.

—2 CORINTHIANS 4:17-18

13 FEBRUARY

Dear Friends,

I am amazed and dismayed every time I pass a bookshelf in our den
these days and realize I have yet to pack away our Advent calendar!
A testament to how busy things have been in the last six weeks since
Christmas.

Every year, on the last night of November, I retrieve from the
garage our wooden Advent calendar and it appears on our family
room mantelpiece on the first of December. There is a tiny door and
cubbyhole for each day of the month. When our son was small, he
had only to figure out which day of the month it was—which numbered door to open—and he would find a chocolate kiss or some
tiny treat inside. But once he learned to read, he found instead simple instructions telling him where to go to find his treat—under the
couch cushion, in a kitchen drawer, in the piano bench or even in
the freezer.

As he grew, the requirements became increasingly demanding.
In the little cubby he might find a clue requiring him to do a math
problem or to play a song on the piano. Sometimes one clue led to
another until he had been all over the house or even through several
computer files before finding what he sought. A trip out to the garage or to a neighbor's mailbox might be called for. But however
demanding the hunt grew, Peter always proceeded willingly and in
good spirits. He knew we wouldn't send him off in pursuit without
first having hidden a treat, and he also was quick to realize that

once we were no longer limited to the small cubbyholes, the treats themselves became larger and more varied.

This seems to me to picture our lives as believers. The Lord's requirements of us seem to intensify as we mature spiritually, but the rewards also grow. The more experience we have with answered prayer and the more we come to know the Lord as trustworthy based on our history together, the more willing we become to venture farther with Him, to attempt new challenges. New areas open up to us in which to be stretched and tested, but also in which to be blessed.

I have heard Praise itself called "a treasure hunt," and it is surely that. Coming to understand each new aspect of God's character inevitably leads to the discovery of another and then another. As our understanding of the Lord grows, our amazement and gratitude and praise also grow. And we thereby become increasingly willing to obey and follow this increasingly amazing Lord.

As life on this earth becomes evermore complicated and painful, I find myself more often thinking of heaven. Yet paradoxically, the more I learn of the promises of *heaven*, the more willing and able I am to tolerate the increasing challenges of life *here*. We can proceed in faith—trusting Him who is our Shepherd and in that reward which is unseen, but sure.

In His Love,
Laura

Our Father in heaven and right here with us, lead on! May we keep in step with You and reach each landmark that You have set for us. May we keep up the fight of faith by trusting in You and

Your good purposes. Keep our eyes on You and our hope alive. In Christ, Amen.

Since, then, you have been raised with Christ, set your hearts
on things above, where Christ is seated at the right hand of God.
Set your mindson things above, not on earthly things.

— COLOSSIANS 2:1-2

20 FEBRUARY

Dear Friends,

"Until last August I had never lost a watch in my life. Then, within ten weeks, I lost not one, not two, but three watches. The last one to go was an expensive gold one but even more importantly it had tremendous sentimental value. It didn't do its job any better than the $24 plastic sports watch I'd lost a month earlier, but I have felt its loss more keenly . . ."

That was the start of a prayer letter I began last fall but never finished. I knew I had a great metaphor for something spiritual, I just wasn't sure what it was. Today I began another:

Despite my love for God and my trust in Him, I haven't been able to bear the thought of losing my brother Nick. His blood counts are so low they have had to stop all treatment. And yet last Wednesday, when I asked Nick how we can best be praying for him, his response amazed and humbled me. He said his greatest challenge after two months in the hospital is discouragement. In his words:

"Yesterday was a hard day. It was just hard. But I know when I feel that way if I can pray and try to get the mind of the Lord, it's always better. Yesterday I was doing my own thing, trying to keep busy. But when I get up and pray and try to read the Word and try to praise Him, the day goes better . . .

"It's so unnatural for us as human beings to want to be on our knees. It's so contrary to who we are. But God is faithful . . . This is new terrain for me, too. The first seven weeks in the hospital I tried to rely on Him, but I realize now I was just trying to stay busy that way . . . I need to draw close to the Lord. I want a deeper worship time. I want to learn a deep praising of God. If I can do that, that's going to be the answer right there. Deeper praise . . . This is a learning experience . . . Something special in the spiritual realm is happening."

Indeed! Nick, living in an isolation room and visited most often by wrens and hummingbirds outside his window, is seeking ways to more deeply praise and worship God.

While I, healthy and active and able to be up and out each day, have managed little more these last two weeks than crying jags and despondency.

This morning my husband said something in prayer about this period in Nick's life being "the passage to glory," and what an illuminating phrase that has been for me. All these weeks that Nick has spent seemingly isolated have been not punishment but a time of preparation. The Father Nick knows and trusts is drawing him close. He is lovingly preparing Nick—and every one of us throughout our lives—not for loss or departure but for arrival! For glory! For home!

Last week at the gym, my sports watch unexpectedly turned up in the Lost and Found. It was one of the three I have lost lately. Tonight, as I moved a box in my closet, there was the gold watch I have missed and mourned since October. Not gone forever as I had feared, but only for a time. Restored to me and more beautiful than I remember, more precious and treasured than ever before.

> With you in Him,
> Laura

Heavenly Father, herald of new life, continue Your work in my heart. Lift my eyes and my desires and my thoughts from the Here and Now. Give me the courage to choose You, to trust You, to keep praying even when I am afraid. For Your glory. Amen.

Let us not be like the others, who are asleep,
but let us be alert and self-controlled.

— 1 THESSALONIANS 5:6

27 FEBRUARY

Dear Friends,

My brother Toby and I met up recently in northern California for a brief visit. The night before our reunion, both of us went to bed in our respective homes and set our alarm clocks so we could get up early for our flights.

When my alarm clock woke me, it wasn't with the usual sound of talk radio or music. Neither was it the annoying beep of the clock's alarm setting. This was something else, and my husband scrambled to silence the insistent honking that had woken us so rudely. By the time we were fully awake he was at our window watching two arguing ducks that had made a landing on our pool. I rolled over as he headed downstairs to shoo the ducks off to another meeting site, and both of us gratefully slept two more hours.

Back in North Carolina, Toby had gone to bed at nine P.M. and woke when his alarm went off. He showered and shaved slowly, feeling exhausted. Just before dressing he glanced at the clock and saw that it was ten o'clock . . . at night! He had been asleep for one hour. The sound that had woken him was not his alarm clock but his telephone, which had rung twice and then stopped. Like Kosta and me thousands of miles away, back to bed he went.

Any number of things may call us from sleep but only one thing calls us to faith. After perhaps years of dullness and false thinking His voice alone calls us to wakefulness and true life. He also is the initiator of every one of our prayers. Recognizing His call to prayer and responding quickly are part of our deepening relationship with Him.

- His call to prayer may be a call to work—to cover someone

He knows is in need. *My servant Job will pray for you and I will accept his prayer.* (Job 42:8)

• His call to prayer may be a call to blessing. *Call to me and I will answer you and tell you great and unsearchable things you do not know.* (Jeremiah 33:3)

• His call to prayer may be a call to share in a confidence as one of His intimates. *Then the Lord said, "Shall I hide from Abraham what I am about to do?"* (Genesis 18:17) *He takes the upright into His confidence.* (Proverbs 3:32)

• His call to prayer may be a call to conviction and confession and cleansing. *If we confess our sins, he is faithful and just and will forgive us our sins and purify us from all unrighteousness.* (1 John 1:9)

Amidst the cacophony of voices coming at us there is only One that matters. His is the voice that steadies us; His is the voice of Truth that drowns out the honk honk honking of this world-that-is-not-our-home. He has planned where He will use you and how He will bless you. Take yourself to prayer. Quiet yourself to listen for His blessing and His leading and His remonstrance and His love. Give it the time it requires. Give Him the time He deserves.

With You in Him,

Laura

Holy One, May I discern Your voice above all others. Lead me in confession and in praise and in service. Deafen me to the voices of condemnation that surely are not Yours but open my ears to Your voice of conviction. May I be willing to hear and respond to what You have to say to me and about me. For Your honor and glory. Amen.

Put out into deep water and let down the nets for a catch

— LUKE 5:4

6 MARCH

Dear Friends,

Each of us needs to spend time alone with God each day. Not because we 'should' or 'must,' but because this is the means by which He makes Himself known to us and advises and blesses and steers us. This is our peace.

Someone asked me recently to describe my daily prayer time. She wanted some fresh ideas to incorporate into what had become a somewhat unsatisfying routine. It can be encouraging and helpful to share with each other what we have found personally useful. We don't hesitate to swap favorite books or parenting tips, but when it comes to our devotional lives we are often less forthcoming. It seems a private topic. Our quiet time is usually spent alone, and we might even wonder if we are 'doing it right.' But our life with God is a love relationship, not religious ritual. And since the aim in our daily quiet time is to know Him better, there are three basics that will help.

Certainly we pray continuously as we go about our daily tasks. But we are talking now about that portion of the day that we devote to Him exclusively. This is the daily set time that is our alone time together. Every relationship needs that time, and this one most of all. It needs to be time that is unhurried and taken when our mind is rested and receptive. For me it is first thing in the morning when I am at my most alert, and before the requirements of the day have sapped my time and energy. And incidentally, we never will feel we have time for this. The time must be taken for it, designated as His and kept inviolate. We don't tend to miss meals, at least not for long. We set a daily time to feed our bodies. And we need to set a regular daily time to feed our spirits.

We also need a quiet place where we can literally close the door and be alone with Him. Intimacy grows not in a crowd but in private moments, and time spent alone with God is where our relationship will deepen and strengthen and our faith take solid root. He has so much He would say to each of us and only awaits our receptive, undistracted attention.

Prayer is conversation with God, and the Bible is His part of that conversation. So our third requirement is a Bible. Reading the Bible is the listening part of prayer. The Bible is called the Word of God and this is where His personal word to us will come. We may be involved in an organized Bible study, a group study perhaps, but this is something else. In this prayerful time of reading our focus is not the Book but the Author of the Book and the Author of our faith.

There may be devotional books we like to read or music we like to listen to as part of our devotional time too. There are numerous options. But whatever else we may add to our time alone with God, these three are the bedrock: the set time, the place of solitude and our Bible.

Each of us will be uniquely led and blessed in this daily, growing, deepening conversation with our living, loving Father. The God Who created and formed us takes the lead in our getting to know Him better. The important thing is to recognize distractions and diversions for what they are and to resolutely refuse to allow anything rob Him and us of that daily time together.

In Him,
Laura

Father, too often I allow my moods or appointment book to steal what is rightly Yours—my time and attention. Thank You for this gift of prayer, for the personal Word You would speak to me. May Your Holy Spirit open my eyes as I read and open my ears as You speak and guide my prayers. In Christ's name. Amen.

Did not your father have food and drink? He did what was
right and just, so all went well with him. He defended the cause
of the poor and needy, and so all went well. Is that not what
it means to know Me?" declares the LORD.

—JEREMIAH 22:15-16

13 MARCH

Dear Friends,

I spoke tonight to a friend in the Midwest. She was commenting on the great challenges she is seeing of late in the lives of believing friends and family. I certainly have been painfully aware of it myself. How often the phone has rung since Christmas with news of a crisis. Why had I thought it was happening only here?

"God is driving His people to their knees," she said, and something in her words struck me with force. That is exactly what is happening. I have felt it keenly in recent months. Have you? A restlessness I could not quite identify. A sense of urgency. It is an insistent and specific call to believers to be in fervent prayer.

A speaker I heard recently talked about the loud wake-up calls God has allowed in recent years both to our nation and to our planet—the September 11th bombings, the Indian Ocean tsunami, Hurricane Katrina. We would be foolish not to heed them. If we believe His Word about what is ahead, if we look around us at the state of our culture and the state of the world, if we acknowledge ourselves as His—here as His body and for His holy purpose of reconciling the world to Him before it is too late—we must take our prayer work very seriously.

God is calling us to the discipline of sustained, fervent prayer. Sometimes we obey, but sometimes we merely nod in agreement only to wander off on our own self-important business. We seem to be talking so much more to each other than we are to Him. We seem to be talking so much more about what we believe than demonstrating that belief through obedience.

I have been thinking this week about self discipline and its opposite, self indulgence. How practiced I have become at indulging my emotions, my whims, my desire to be admired or fed well or entertained. But He is calling us to prayer, and He has called some of us lately, loudly, through pain—what C.S. Lewis so rightly has called "God's megaphone."

My friend's comment came at just the moment I needed it—a reminder of God's intentionality and kingship. I must think beyond my narrow circle of cares and heartaches and remember that God is mightily at work on a much larger scale than I tend to think of, and for a much greater purpose. After our conversation tonight I had to ask myself what I have been waiting for. There is a lot of praying to do. He has entrusted it to us and He is relying on us for it. It is a large part of why we are here.

> With love,
> Laura

Father, guide my prayers. Bring to my mind all the things and people You are expecting me to cover in prayer. May the conversation between You and me be continuous and purposeful. May it accomplish all that You intend and lead to Your greater glory. In Christ's name. Amen.

The word of the Lord came to Jonah son of Amittai:
"Go to the great city of Nineveh . . ." But Jonah ran away
from the LORD and headed for Tarshish . . .

— JONAH 1:1-3

20 MARCH

Dear Friends,

More and more lately, as I have said before, I have felt called to be in prayer. There is no seeming end to the loved ones and situations that need to be handed over to God's care.

Yesterday I learned that a friend has cancer and perhaps only a year to live. He and his family are in particular need of comfort and care right now. So I set aside some time in the evening to pray for them very specifically. I had only just begun praying when my son appeared and invited me to watch a movie with him. He'd been out all day and we had a chance now to be together.

It was late, after 11, and I was tired. I eyed the clock and hesitated. But since I had not had much time with Pete since he got home from college for Spring Break, I gave in and joined him downstairs. Prayer time shelved. Sleep deferred.

I was ninety minutes into the movie before my growing unease finally erupted into an unavoidable and awful conviction that I was not where I was supposed to be. I excused myself and went back upstairs to pray, briefly, and then to sleep. This morning I overslept and missed church. So that unsettled feeling lingered of not being where I knew I was supposed to be.

Pete had no need for more TV last night. And the time we spent together in silence watching a movie would have been far better invested in sleep for him and prayer for me, and would have netted us time in the car this morning to talk as we drove to church, and a rare chance to worship together. Instead, both of us dragged out of bed late, squinting against the brightness of a beautiful day. I had chosen the good and missed the best.

When we are tempted to step away from something God has asked us to do and equipped us to do and given us the desire to do, the temptation does not come to us in the form of a creepy, ominous stranger with red eyes and a pitchfork in his hand. It comes to us as the most attractive, appealing prospect we can imagine. For me, some time with my loved child. But the time I took with him was stolen from elsewhere, from something I knew I was supposed to be doing.

We have innumerable options at any given moment of where we can be and what we can be doing. Many of them are appealing and many are good. But the place of blessing and real power is where God is at work and where He intends to include us and to make use of us. And only He can tell us where that is, so we need those periods of quiet time with Him, we need to cultivate a still and listening heart sensitive to His steering. But even if we get the message, we can get diverted. And when the realization comes that we are not where He would have us be, we need to confess it and ask His help to move back into alignment with what He would have us do. It is never too late, and though we may be regretful at our delay, we can return to Him at a run, thankful, thankful for His faithfulness to our loved ones when we fail them and for His forgiveness and for His power to redeem.

With you in prayer,

Laura

Gracious heavenly Father, give me the courage to say 'no' when a conflicting voice calls me from what You have asked me to do. I am powerless in my own strength to do so. Amen.

[NOTE: OUR FRIEND WITH CANCER DIED WITHIN DAYS OF THIS, NOT MONTHS AS PREDICTED.]

Blessed is he who has regard for the weak;
the Lord delivers him in times of trouble.

—PSALM 41:1

27 MARCH

Dear Friends,

After missing a shot in an important water polo game, my son angrily yelled at himself, "You idiot!" and was promptly thrown out of the game for misconduct. "I was talking to myself!" he protested to the ref. "You were disrespecting a player in this game. You are a player, are you not?" And out he went.

How do you respond when you miss a shot? Does your reaction take you out of the game? Mine did recently. I had asked the Lord to show me anything in me that needed confessing. And then He did! And I was so surprised and distraught by what He showed me that instead of taking it right to Him in confession, I curled up in shame and for days refused even to look in His direction.

When my eyes dropped from Who God is and settled firmly onto who I am in my sin, my prayer life and effectiveness for the Lord came to a grinding halt. Days later, with eagerness and relief, I was able to hurry to Him in confession only when I remembered that God's love for me is undiminished by my sin; His love for me is not linked to my performance.

If you make a mistake do you get locked into regret? Where do you allow your thoughts to settle? We need to be as quick and careful to force our minds away from dwelling on our confessed sin as we are quick to turn our minds from inappropriate sexual thoughts or hateful thoughts of others. All are equally unworthy of God, all are equally unfaithful and dishonorable to Him.

When the Lord shows us something unlovely in ourselves, it can be tempting to give in to hopelessness or self recrimination or breast beating. But we have to keep our focus on Him and remind ourselves of Who He is. His ways are not our ways. The Lord points out our faults not with the voice of condemnation but with the compassionate intention of empowering us to overcome them. He is reaching out a hand and offering to pull us up to a new level of living without that particular encumbrance. His pointing it out to us now says, "It is time. You are ready to face this. Together, My hand in yours, let's lay it down."

May each revelation of our sin lead us into immediate confession, and then praise at Who He is and at His great love rather than despair over how unfit we are for that love, or how undeserving.

Be faithful to confess. As soon as we do so, He has moved on and He graciously invites us to do the same. Let us not hang back in regret but keep in step with Him Who is our Life.

Amazed in His great love,
Laura

Father, Help me to trust Your love for me and to rest in it. Protect me from the enemy who so longs to entrap me in despair and hopelessness. May I be quick to confess what You bring to my mind and to leave that sin behind as I walk on with You in new life. Amen.

" . . . your will be done on earth as it is in heaven."

—MATTHEW 6:10

3 APRIL

Dear Friends,

When my son was small, he had two friends named Will and Alex. One evening he asked me with some concern, "Why do we always pray for God's will, but we never pray for God's Alex?"

Sometimes God's will is noticeably absent from my prayer list. When there is something I desperately desire, I too often think of prayer as a means to bring God around to my way of thinking, to make my will His. I give Him all the details of the situation (as if He doesn't already know them) and tell Him how important this outcome is to me. I try to make Him see reason. And lest I sound too selfish, I explain why this particular thing would actually be best for all concerned. I imagine that if I am only eloquent or persuasive enough things will go as I want them to.

Sometimes if my prayer isn't answered as I'd hoped, I feel like a fool. Or a failure. I decide I was silly to have hoped. I tell myself I didn't pray hard enough or long enough or with a pure enough motive . . . I decide I didn't make my case convincingly . . . I conclude that God doesn't love me. With that kind of outcome, is it any wonder that I am often hesitant to pray for things that seem very unlikely to happen? That hesitation reflects not only my vanity but a reluctance to "fail."

When faced with a seemingly impossible desire, how do you pray? Do you pray at all or do you simply accede defeat? If you do pray for a highly unlikely outcome, do you pray believing or without real conviction? To avoid "being wrong" or looking foolish, do you instead assess the possible outcomes and simply pray for the one that seems most likely to happen?

Surely no one ever prayed more earnestly for a desired (but unlikely) outcome than Jesus did. On the night He was arrested He asked His Father if He could avoid the cross that was ahead of Him. And how did He ask it? What tone did He take? How did He approach God? He approached Him unhesitatingly as a son to his father and stated His desire simply. But most significant is the way He couched His brief request. Notice how He both prefaced and concluded it:

"Father, if you are willing, take this cup from me; yet not my will, but yours be done."

God's will was, first and last, Jesus' primary desire. He wanted His request granted only if it was in accordance with His Father's will. The unlikelihood of His request being granted did not prevent Him from making it. And when God declined that request I don't imagine it led Jesus to question God's love or to consider Himself betrayed or to feel foolish for having asked.

Prayer is the means by which we share with God our desires and hopes. But by prayer we also express the willingness to yield our will to His. Our will must be that His will be done.

Love,
Laura

Father, we are here as Your agents and Your ambassadors and Your loved ones. Please bring our wills into accord with Your own. May we be willing to trust You even for the impossible, and may we continue to trust regardless of Your answer to our prayers. More and more, may we be willing for Your will be done for us and in us and through us. And Lord, wherever they are, bless and protect Will and Alex. Amen.

I will praise you, O Lord my God, with all my heart;
I will glorify your name forever.

—PSALM 86:12

10 APRIL

Dear Friends,

I was challenged recently when someone asked, "Can you honestly add this phrase to each of your prayers: 'I ask this, God, for Your glory.'" Such a phrase forces me to consider my prayer requests in a new light. It requires me to evaluate my motives. Am I making this request for myself alone or because it will result in glory to God?

Glory to God. What does such a phrase mean? There are words and phrases we use often but might be hard pressed to define if asked to do so. "Glory" is a word used several ways in the Bible but in the context of God's glory it refers to honor and praise that are given to Him and that are His due. To "glorify God" is to render Him praise and honor. Asking something "for God's glory" expresses the hope that the answer to our prayer will result in honor and praise to Him.

How wonderfully this deepens and elevates and expands our prayers. We are making our request not only for the sake of the ones prayed for but for the sake of the larger objective that He Himself may be known, worshipped and praised.

By praising God we can cause Him to be held in greater esteem or respect! That is literally what it means to "magnify the Lord." So our praise has far greater power and more importance than we may realize. Its fruit extends far beyond our own lives. Praise to God does not feed some heavenly ego but accomplishes His loving purpose in this world. As we declare what we know to be true of God, it causes others to lift their eyes to Him and to come to know Who He is.

So we ask what we ask in prayer for God's sake, for the sake of

His loving, holy purposes and objectives, for the sake of His glory. But until we know and love Him, His being honored and praised won't be a matter of particular interest or concern to us. It is vital then that we spend time with Him in conversation and in reading what He has to say about Himself in the Bible. Then our praise will be sincere and rooted in Who we know Him to be. And our knowing and loving Him will bear lasting fruit because it will inevitably result in our praising Him,

which will bring Him honor,

which will increase the joy and praise of others who love Him,

which will bring Him honor,

which will cause those who don't know Him to look up . . .

> With You in His mighty hand,
> Laura

Heavenly Father, Your Word says that Your love toward me is great. May my love toward You be great. May it motivate all that I do. May my choices and decisions be guided by a desire to honor You. For Your great glory. Amen.

There is neither Jew nor Greek, slave nor free, male nor female,
for you are all one in Christ Jesus.

— GALATIONS 3:28

17 APRIL

Dear Friends,

My husband and I arrived at the Boston Museum of Fine Arts one day last week eager to see as much of it as our schedule and our feet would allow. And we did pretty well. But as we began, as we stood in the lobby consulting our map and plotting our course, I was reminded again of our differences—differences based not so much on gender as nationality. My Greek-born husband was pulling toward the right and the Classical gallery while I was eager to head off to the Colonial America collection.

We eventually saw it all, but very differently, I'm sure. I moved a little faster through the Greek sculptures and friezes and coins than my husband did. And I confess to skipping or speed-reading many of the descriptions of the various pieces. Similarly, in the Colonial America exhibits, while I excitedly exclaimed over the Gilbert Stuart portraits and Revere silver, my husband probably was viewing them with as appreciative an eye but with more detachment or objectivity.

Both of us, though, shared the same excitement and emotion and gratitude at the baptisms during our Easter church service the next morning. Two graduate students who came to this country from China a few years ago and came to faith in Christ more recently, shared their personal stories of faith using English that was not entirely intelligible but was deeply felt and understood and celebrated by all of us in their family of believers. And when they were baptized, "in the name of the Father and of the Son and of the Holy Spirit" was spoken in their own Chinese dialect by the Caucasian minister conducting the service. What a moving reminder that the language of Christianity is not English or Aramaic or Greek but the shared language of faith. And our heritage, whatever it may be ethnically or geographically, is the heritage we all share as sinners saved by faith in the same Lord. As the service ended, hundreds of us sang as one powerful voice the words of John Wesley, "Christ the Lord is risen today! Allelujah!"

When we first come to Christ in faith and come forever after in prayer, we come as His loved one. We are expected and welcomed and heard and answered. There is none who is more worthy than another or who more rightly claims a connection or familial tie to Christ. None of us can pull out a family tree to prove a closer link to Him than anyone else. We are all branches that have been grafted in, all adopted sons and daughters. Each of us who prays today is equally undeserving of God's grace but is equally able and grateful and amazed to address Almighty God as "Our Father."

Your sister in Christ,
Laura

Heavenly Father, for the gift of Your Son, we thank You. For opening a way for us to come to You, we thank You. For our salvation, for our adoption as Yours, we thank You. May Your name be honored and lifted in praise and with reverence. For Your glory. Amen

Therefore every scribe who has been trained for the
kingdom of heaven is like a master of a house,
who brings out of his treasure what is new and what is old.

— MATTHEW 13:52

24 APRIL

Dear Friends,

I recently found a gift certificate in my wallet, forgotten since Christmas. So last Wednesday I went and picked out a new skirt and two tops for summer. But when I stepped into my closet to hang them up, I looked around and could only wonder what I had been thinking. The last thing I needed was more clothes. Going through the hanging clothes, I began to lay aside those things that were worn out or no longer fit or hadn't been worn in a couple of years. The pile grew.

The clean sweep went on all week. Even my husband got into the act and added clothes of his own to the pile. The great discovery turned out to be the existing treasure in my closet—clothes that fit well and that I like. Clothes already mine that I'd forgotten. All winter I'd worn the same two pairs of pants because it was easier just to grab what I knew would work than to search out alternatives in the jumble. But it turns out I have several pairs that fit. Once the clutter was cleared away I rediscovered a lot of goodies.

So despite the bags of clothes in our hallway that are on their way out, I feel not loss but gain. Where once there was disorder and a confusing myriad of options, I now have a closet of clean clothes in my size. There are fewer clothes, but I actually have a more varied wardrobe because my eye and mind can take in the reduced number of options and make choices. Best of all, other people will benefit from what has hung unused in our closet for so long.

Clutter can be a great threat to our prayer lives and spiritual lives as well. There's so much coming at us, so many options, that it can be hard to focus. Inspirational radio as we drive to Bible study; praise music playing at home; study guides, retreat tapes and prayer plans pile up on our desks or tabletops; commentaries, concordances, the latest Christian bestseller that we're sure is going to change our lives. My bookshelves hold numerous unread or once-read books that I'm unlikely to read again that could be in the hands of someone eager to make use of them.

I long to pare down and zoom in on what I already own, to live out and share those spiritual truths that I've taken in so far. Besides, 1 Corinthians 12:7 tells us that our gifts were given to us not just for ourselves but "for the common good." We have been blessed with abundance and both our material and spiritual gifts need to be out there in use. Keep them moving! Share the wealth.

Our lives with Christ are intended to be light, bright—blessed, not burdened. Unhurried conversation, whispered communion, not a slog through piles of "stuff." Once we simplify we'll undoubtedly rediscover forgotten treasures already ours.

He who takes great delight in you has something to say. Something just for you, just for today. Clear a spot. Settle down. Quiet yourself.

> With you in Him,
> Laura

Speak, Lord, for your servant is listening. Amen

*You show that you are a letter from Christ . . . written not
with ink but with the Spirit of the living God, not on tablets
of stone but on tablets of human hearts.*

—2 CORINTHIANS 3:3

1 MAY. May Day.

Dear Friends,

I think Mrs. Wilson's second grade classroom was the first place I
heard about May baskets—spring flowers nested among grasses or
leaves or moss in a woven construction paper basket and left anony-
mously at the front doors of loved ones. I was delighted with the
idea of leaving something beautiful and unexpected and unearned
on someone's doorstep.

My husband recently gave me just such a gift. He and I had had
Round 1,058 of a disagreement I have been resurrecting since 1983.
I said very mean things that morning. By afternoon, an infection
that had been brewing in my head and chest had become a horrible
flu and strep throat. By evening, high fever and weakness kept me
from walking or even reaching for a Kleenex without help. And my
husband, with every reason to keep his distance both physically and
emotionally, tenderly met every need I had, and he continued to do
so over several days and nights. His unhesitating, loving care was
wholly undeserved, and my contrite heart could only thank him
and marvel at so tangible an enactment of grace.

Running around doing errands one day last week, I was feeling
down and a bit dry spiritually. So I abandoned my plans and drove
home. I realized that time with God was my most pressing errand,
and that nothing was going to be quite right until I did what I most
needed to do. So I sat in my chair by the window and had a sweet
time of prayer and confession and reunion. And afterward I opened
my Bible to God's promise in Jeremiah 31:34, *For I will forgive their
wickedness and remember their sins no more.* Words that were a de-

light to my eyes. Beautiful, unexpected, unearned. A May basket from God.

Last night the idea dropped into my mind to write a letter of love to someone who has hurt me undeservedly. In prickly, difficult relationships distance and silence can be a relief, and preferable to painful contact. But there is another option, there is unmerited kindness—lovely, unanticipated. And I learned again that delivering a May basket can be as satisfying as receiving one.

Whenever we bypass the inclinations of our naturally thorny hearts and reach beyond them to kindness, to a generous gesture, to anything redolent of Christ, our victory is a gift to God—a vivid, joy-inducing, fragrant offering delivered to the doorstep of heaven.

With love,
Laura

O Lord! For the colors and sweetness with which you surround us, for your forgiveness so freely given, for your smiling welcome when we drag in, yet again, with so much to confess to You, we thank you! You are holy, and we are not. You are pure love and life and our doorway to both. Continue to teach us, to insist on Your way. Do not let us peacefully walk our wayward paths apart from You. Keep drawing us back. For Your glory and praise. Amen

All the streams flow into the sea, yet the sea is never full.
To the place the streams come from, there they return again.

— ECCLESIASTES 1:7

8 MAY

Dear Friends,

My husband's area of professional expertise is flash flooding. (Mitigating against it not causing it!) One of the most surprising things I've learned from him is that virtually no new water is ever created. All the water that God created in the beginning just keeps getting recycled in an elegant system called the hydrologic cycle. Rain falls on the earth and runs in rivulets and rivers into the seas. The sun warms the seas, and the water evaporates and rises as vapor to form clouds. As the vapor cools, it becomes liquid again and falls to the earth as rain. What a picture of God's creative genius and economy.

Many hundreds of years before science recognized and understood this cycle it was described in Ecclesiastes and in Job, perhaps the oldest book in the Bible. Job 36:27-28 says, *He draws up the drops of water, which distill as rain to the streams; the clouds pour down their moisture and abundant showers fall on mankind.*

And then there is Isaiah, beautiful Isaiah. *As the rain and the snow come down from heaven and do not return to it without watering the earth and making it bud and flourish, so that it yields seed for the sower and bread for the eater, so is my word that goes out from my mouth. It will not return to me empty, but will accomplish what I desire and achieve the purpose for which I sent it.* (Isaiah 55:10-11).

Comparing it to rain, we are told several exciting truths here about God's Word—that it is sent to earth for a purpose, that it will achieve that purpose, that it is sent by God and that His Word will return to Him as rain waters do.

Certainly we know that Jesus (*"the Word"* according to John) accomplished the purpose for which He was sent before returning to His Father. Scripture is also God's Word, which He loves. And I wonder if our weaving His Word through our prayers sweetens the aroma of our offering to Him.

Including scripture in our prayers is something we already do, often without even realizing it. Every time we praise God by any of His biblical names or titles we are praying scripture. Anytime we claim a specific promise of God for a loved one, we are praying His Word back to Him. Do you ever insert your child's name in a verse and pray that verse for him or her? It is a practice I highly recommend. Jesus' own prayers often included scripture, even on the cross. *Into Your hands I commit my spirit,* is Psalm 31:5. *My God, my God, why have you forsaken me?* is also one of David's prayers— Psalm 22:1.

God's Word will return to Him. He will never allow it to fall to the ground. What better way for the *words of my mouth and the meditation of my heart [to] be pleasing in His sight* (Psalm 19:14) than for my words to be His.

With you in the Word,

Laura

Lord Jesus, we praise You as the wisdom of God and the power of God. Sanctify us by the truth; Your word is truth. To You be honor and might forever. Amen.

But thanks be to God, who always leads us in triumphal procession
in Christ and through us spreads everywhere the fragrance of the
knowledge of him. For we are to God the aroma of Christ among
those who are being saved and those who are perishing.

— 2 CORINTHIANS 2:14–15

15 MAY

Dear Friends,

At Biola University, before the fall semester begins, each incoming freshman is asked to submit the recipe for their favorite dish of their mom's. One night at a time the cafeteria staff cooks each freshman's favorite for the entire student body. When it's your turn, your name is displayed on a large blackboard by the food line. Imagine walking into the dining hall one night during your first year away from home and smelling your favorite dish cooking—the aroma that most means home to you.

2 Corinthians 2:15 says something thrilling to those who have accepted His forgiveness—that to God Himself we are the aroma of Christ! We are the aroma of that which God most loves, that which most means home to God.

At the very start of the Bible, Noah makes a sacrifice to God and *the LORD smelled the pleasing aroma* (Genesis 8:21). Near the end of the Bible, John describes golden bowls in heaven *full of incense, which are the prayers of the saints.* (Revelation 5:8). Our ongoing prayers rise to Him, sweet-smelling. Our time spent serving Him, a sacrifice of time and energy, is also a pleasing aroma to the Lord. Don't fall into the trap, though, of thinking that our value to God lies solely in what we do for Him.

When our service to Him is interrupted by illness or suspended for some other reason, we face the danger of thinking of ourselves as less valuable or of lesser worth to Him. I have felt that way. But remember that to God we are the aroma of His Son both when we are actively serving Him and when we are not, when we are praying and when we forget to pray or fail to pray or don't want to pray. Serving or sitting, gracious or annoyed, we are His—not because of what we do, but because of Who He is.

This morning at the pool, a dad was teaching his young son to swim. The little boy, was crying and scared. "I can't! I can't breathe! Don't let go!" And his father reminded him, "You were swimming like a champ last summer. Remember? You know this stuff!" The child knew it a year ago but summer is nearly here and he needs to relearn what he once knew. And so do we.

We who work together in the leadership of Community Bible Study will lay down that service this week and begin our summertime break. Some are worried about becoming inconsistent in their devotional time over the summer without the discipline of weekly study and shared prayer time. But one each of us can hold our own spiritually. We just need to relearn that we can, and we will. And of course we aren't really alone—our Father is with us.

It's time for a new kind of service. It's time to get out our flip flops and polish them up for a summer of beach walks and family time. Walk on with the Lord, in the Lord, for the Lord. Send your sweet prayers up to Him throughout your days and nights. In gratitude, in need, in praise, in confession, may the conversation continue and deepen and rise to bless the heart of Him to whom you are the aroma of home.

> With you in heart and
> with you in Him,
> Laura

Almighty God, May You be honored. May You be glorified, Amen.

...

Year Two

...

My purpose in writing is to encourage you and to assure you
that the grace of God is with you no matter what happens.

— 1 PETER 5:12

4 SEPTEMBER

Dear Friends,

There is a long letter in my computer that I wrote back in June. I
worked on it for days and watched it grow and grow. I was very
pleased with parts of it and less so with others. But the letter was
never sent. Or, I should say, delivered. It was intended for my un-
suspecting son, home from college for the summer and just down
the hall. Three weeks after his arrival I had amassed quite a collection of things I wanted to talk to him about, impressions I wanted
to share. I just knew he would welcome my advice and soak up my
wisdom and savor my perspective on his life and tastes . . .

Thankfully, Peter was spared. The Lord stopped me with an
unexpected word and a much needed reminder: "My part is to convict. Yours is to pray."

My part is to pray. That truth has come back to me over and
over all summer long. My son is near twenty and now more than
ever, as a mother, my part is to pray—from great distances or just
down the hall. My voice in Pete's ear does not carry the weight it
once did. And I never could do more than convince anyway. And
whatever I can talk him into, someone else can talk him out of.

The Lord's voice, though, does more than convince. It convicts.
His is the voice of truth. And He is asking me to trust Him to say to
Peter what Peter needs to hear. His part is to convict. My part is to
pray.

With the coming of autumn a new year of ministry is beginning
for many of us. We stand ready in these first days excited and perhaps apprehensive about new roles or assignments. But He is not
asking any of us to take on more than He has assigned. And He will

equip us for His assignment. Remember that our part in His work is neither to preach nor to convince nor to perform. Our part, chiefly, is to pray. We will pray and we will stand back and watch Him work. We will watch Him convict and lead and accomplish every one of His purposes for this world. We will pray and we will watch Him bring about His highest good.

The will of our Sovereign God will be done, we need not doubt that. It will be done and it will be a glorious display. And as intercessors He has offered us front row seats.

With You in Christ,
Laura

Our Father, we wait and we watch with hope and excitement. We thank You today for all You have planned for the season ahead. Work in the hearts of each of us what only You can. Guide us in laying down any worry, any work, that is not from You. We praise You as our King. Amen.

I have stilled and quieted my soul.

—PSALM 131:2

11 SEPTEMBER

Dear Friends,

I was listening to a tape of a favorite Bible teacher one day last summer. Later in the day, resuming the tape, I was maddened by how much I already had forgotten.

"Lord, don't let all this good teaching go to waste! Please rule over my increasingly poor memory. Remind me of what I heard. Let it sink in more deeply."

Instead He reminded me of something far more important than whatever the radio teacher had been sharing. John 14:26 is what came to my mind. *The Counselor, the Holy Spirit . . . will remind you of everything I have said to you.* The Holy Spirit Himself will remind me of everything Jesus has said to me. None of it will be lost, despite my sluggish gray matter.

But I also heard in that verse a truth I had never heard before. "The Holy Spirit will remind you of everything I have said to you! Not to the teacher on the radio. Not to your pastor. Not to your more scholarly friend. To you. That's all that matters between Me and you."

I need not keep up with every Christian bestseller or frantically scribble notes while listening to teaching tapes or radio, afraid of missing a key point. What is most important for me personally is what Jesus has for me personally. And He will make sure I get that. It comes to me through His Word, it comes in prayer, it come through the teaching of others and the counsel of godly friends. The Holy Spirit will remind me of all the things that matter for me and my life and my sanctification. I have His Word on that.

When we accepted Christ's forgiveness, each of us embarked with Him on a completely individualized course of instruction. He knows what we most need to learn, to surrender, to hear. Who better than He to realize all the plans and purposes He had in creating each of us? Who better to refine and shape me into the finished Laura that only He can see? No one is more committed to that process. Not even me.

He will tell each of us what we most need to hear. Over and over, if necessary. We need not worry that we will miss or forget it. Our part is to be listening for His voice. For me that has meant driving with the radio off much of the time. It has meant ensuring there are quiet stretches in my day when I am actively listening for His instruction, correction, reassurance. The Lord has a very personal word and counsel for each one of us.

As you read His Word this week and as you pray, listen for Him. What He has to say to you and wants to say to you is what matters most.

Trusting Him with you,
Laura

Lord God Almighty, guide me in all things. Speak to me, lead me. May I trust in You and Your plan for my life. Thank you for all Your sweet promises to me. In Christ's name, Amen.

Fear not, for behold, I bring you good tidings of great joy.

— LUKE 2:10

18 SEPTEMBER

Dear Friends,

My wedding day was surely a joyous one, but I have lived ever since with one abiding and great regret. Just before he walked me down the aisle, my father turned to me, took my hands in his and started to say something. Sentimentalist that he was, I have no doubt he had planned something eloquent and heartfelt to say to his only daughter at such a moment. I was in such a state of nerves, however, and so afraid of losing control of myself, that I cut him off and insisted that he not say a word.

"But, honey, . ."

"No, no, no. Please!"

He complied, but with obvious regret.

How I wish I had allowed my poor dad to have his say! As it turned out, my nerves prevailed in any case. Tears had begun coursing down my cheeks before I even took my first step down the aisle seconds later, so refusing to let him speak had spared me nothing. And I robbed us both of something precious.

I have been robbing God of something precious. And I didn't realize it until recent months when I began to set aside the first part of each day for extended prayer and quiet time. Quiet time. For years my days have begun in prayer, and He surely knows the sound of my voice—my chatter is unceasing. New, though, have been silence and stillness and waiting. New has been the sound of His voice to me.

Only in quiet does that voice break through. What He has to say is too important, too personal to be shouted. And He has required my full attention. So He has waited for His moment. He has waited. I think this is something for which He has waited all my life. And this summer, at last, I began to allow it. Daily He turns me to Himself and He takes my hands in His and He speaks to me.

I have let fear stop me. I have waited, and have wasted so many mornings. What have I feared? Losing control? He controls all things. Welling up? The tears come, and they are welcome. Tears of wonderment and gratitude, conviction and awe. His voice is as tender as a father's to his cherished daughter.

I had a brief note from a friend last week. She's doing well, she reports. She's been listening to a lot of good teaching tapes, praying a lot, reading the Bible, memorizing Scripture. With all that, though, something is missing. "I still need to stop avoiding sitting down and being quiet so He can speak to me. I guess I'm a little scared."

I have been more than a little scared. But we have nothing to fear. My happy surprise this summer has been that He speaks what we most long to hear. He Himself put that longing in our hearts just so He could have this moment between us—bringing to his daughter the word she most needs.

Do not delay His joy or your blessing.

> With you in Him,
> Laura

May I bless You today, Father, with stillness and silence. Speak to my heart. Amen.

The world and its desires pass away,
but the man who does the will of God lives forever.

— 1 JOHN 2:15

25 SEPTEMBER

Dear Friends,

Confession is not typically a part of my time with friends, but I have a confession to make: I covet Peggy's singing voice. I envy Joyce's smile. I want Pat's shoes and Althea's gentle spirit. I am itching to have Betty Jo's joie de vivre and Janet's braid and Mary's grandson. I want Sandy's composure and Marlene's house. I am here but I want to be there. I have my dad's nose but I would prefer his thin thighs. I have my mother's emotional nature but I have always wanted her beautiful hands. And the litany goes on. And it degenerates into a list so petty and greedy that I would be ashamed for you to see it.

A couple of days last week I was exceedingly grouchy and malcontented. I didn't want what I had—I wanted what he had, what she had. I didn't want company, I wanted to be alone. I didn't want unending solitude; where did everybody go? Nothing satisfied. And the Lord finally gave me a good talking to. (Do they still use that expression?) He set me straight and lifted my eyes and spirits.

He spoke not of me, but of Him. He reminded me of what I'm here for and what I'm not, what will last and what will not, what matters and what does not. His tone was a gracious one, more gracious than I deserve. He speaks more kindly to me than I speak to myself.

"Lift your eyes off the earthly realm," He nudged me. "What I'm doing is what matters. Take the long view." Our eyes get locked on the horizontal plane and He wants to raise our sights. He whispers reminders of all that's going on behind the scenes, off the earthly stage. He wants us to glimpse all those chariots on the hills that He showed to Elisha's servant. (2 Kings 6:17).

Years ago I edited a book on Alzheimer's disease that described a condition called downward restricted gaze. In time, Alzheimer's patients lose their peripheral vision and, later still, their eyes become locked in a downward gaze. Doesn't that sound like what can happen to us spiritually? At times our peripheral vision dims and we fail to consider or even remember the people around us and their needs. My gaze last week was surely a restricted and downward one. Locked, in fact, on my own dull self and my desires and demands.

"Eyes Front!" the U.S. Army hollers at its troops. "Eyes up!" commands our Chief.

> With You in Him,
> Laura

Loved Lord, Thank You for Your mercy and persistence in drawing us back on track and back to Your side when we wander off into nonsense and selfishness. You are everlasting and true. Keep our eyes on You. Keep our ears alert to Your voice. Keep our feet quick to follow. We ask this for our safety and for Your glory. Amen.

. . . in His word I put my hope.

—PSALM 130:5

2 OCTOBER

Dear Friends,

What I was looking for? I no longer remember. But one evening last spring I struck gold online. I discovered that a college library has in its collection forty pages of letters written by my mother between 1955 and 1966, the year she died. The letters were written to a cousin, an alumnus of the school, who bequeathed her papers to the library years ago.

I contacted the library the next morning and copies of the letters arrived at my house within days. That night, after everyone was asleep, I sat alone on our bathroom floor leaning against the tub, looking at my mother's handwriting, reading the letters, and studying the photographs of myself and my three brothers that were included.

Who could have imagined that hidden away in a college library were descriptions, among other things, of a December morning when I was six years old and making Christmas cookies with my mother. I read those letters with eagerness and excitement and gratitude. I read them as a daughter hungry since the age of nine for the sound of her mother's voice. Here were her thoughts on some of her struggles. Here were her humor and one of her recipes. She was planning, she said, to take me on a trip to Texas in the spring of 1964 to visit her family. Did we go? I heard her first impressions of Bob Dylan ("such a talented boy") and the way she thought motherhood was best approached. I learned more about who my mother was. I learned more about who I am.

But others will likely read those letters. An eager college freshman might read them as assigned homework. She might peruse them anxiously, afraid of missing whatever the professor intended her to see. A graduate student might reference them if they support his thesis topic. A social critic or historian studying American suburban life in the 1950's and 1960's might cite them. Each of us will read them differently.

It occurs to me that how we approach the Bible reveals a lot about how we regard our relationship with its Author. And our objective in opening that Book largely determines (and can limit) what we find there. Is it the necessary but dry assigned reading for a Bible study we're a part of? Is it a work of literature that we admire with some detachment for its beautiful language and poetry? Is it a valuable historic document that has much to tell us of ancient Israel and Judah? Is it a collection of love letters to you from your Father?

It is possible, even for us who know and love Him, for the Bible to become something we reach for with some weariness or resignation because we know we "should." We forget what a treasure it is that we have in our hands. This is where He speaks to us. This is where that Father voice comes to us with love and counsel.

When you open it, every time you open it, ask the Holy Spirit to guide you. Ask Him to lead you and to open your eyes and your ears to just the word He has for you, loved child.

In Him,
Laura

Thank You for Your Word to me. May I honor You with my reverence for it and obedience to it. Thank You that Your Word is living and active. Thank You, Father, that You are living and active! Amen.

"Yes, Lord," he said, "you know that I love you."
Jesus said, "Feed my lambs."

—JOHN 21:17

9 OCTOBER

Dear Friends,

I am recently back from a visit with my in-laws in Greece. Some evenings, while there is still light, my mother-in-law and I walk. We make our way down to the water and sit a while.

All along the way we come upon hungry cats. Some freeze at the sight of us, others run away. They are wild and untrusting. I carry a bag of dry cat food in my pocket on our walks. When I see a cat, I pour a little mound of food on the road and move away. They won't approach as long as I am between them and the food.

In more than two decades of visiting that neighborhood I have never gone walking by myself, and I have good reason. Yes, there are needy cats along the way, but there are also dogs. Not the tail-wagging, hopeful, friendly pets I know back home; these are German shepherds and rottweilers, trained guard dogs. Up and down the dusty road, snarling dogs protect their patch, and I am intruder. Many are kept behind walls and fences, some are chained, but several are loose and in the road. And all of them bark and growl. No matter how I prepare myself as I approach that black gate down the way, the sudden threatening snarl of the black mastiff always makes me nearly jump out of my shoes. The scene has been played over and over and is always a source of great amusement to my mother-in-law.

This is no place for a relaxing stroll, and were it not for the beauty of the beach sunset or the hungry cats along the way I would likely stay home. A walk takes resolve and I steel myself for it. One needs to be on guard and to proceed as my five-foot-tall mother-in-law does—with an air of command and confidence. When dogs approach she laughs at them and makes fun of their threats. She marches past them as if she owns the road. She doesn't speak English and likely has never heard Teddy Roosevelt's admonition to "walk softly and carry a big stick." Nevertheless she carries her stick and unhesitatingly makes her way through the midst of them. She knows her position in relation to the dogs. She never bows to their noise or flinches at it. And they recognize her fearlessness and allow her to pass.

Studying God's Word we are making our way to the water. Sharing God's Word we carry food to the hungry. And challenges inevitably will come because we have committed to do so. That's why we are wise to walk alongside more spiritually mature companions who know the way and who walk the road with an air of ownership. Threats and growls and sudden snarls come from the most unexpected places. But thanks be to God, our pockets are not empty. Neither are we alone. We do not wander aimlessly. And we brave what frightens us in order to feed those who need what we bring. Anticipating the colors of that sunset, we refill our pockets and proceed with confidence and

in Christ,
Laura

Holy One, go before me, go with me, follow behind. Quiet my fears so that the loudest voice in my ear is neither my own, nor some other's growl, but Your Voice leading me onward.

In Jesus' name. Amen.

When your words came, I ate them; they were my joy and
my heart's delight, for I bear your name.

—JEREMIAH 15:16

16 OCTOBER

Dear Friends,

If you went into a Greek café and asked for "toast and a Coke"
would you be surprised when the waiter brought you a grilled ham
and cheese sandwich and a chocolate pastry? That's what would
happen. We hear or use words thinking we understand their mean-
ing but the truth can be a delicious surprise.

I called myself a "Christian" all my life not knowing the mean-
ing of the word. I was in my thirties before a friend opened the
Bible and explained to me what Jesus was doing on the cross. He
was paying the debt for my sins. He came to earth for that purpose.
He was taking my punishment and securing my complete forgiveness—something I would never be able to do for myself. I had been
in church all my life, but this was news to me. In thirty-one years of
sermons and chatter no one had ever spelled out the simple truth.

But even learning all that didn't make me a Christian. Something was required on my part. I had to admit I needed what Jesus
did for me. And I did that in a brief prayer. I acknowledged my sin
and I thanked Him for doing what only He could do. I accepted
His gift of forgiveness.

I read a helpful analogy this week. We know when we get married. It doesn't just happen. We can look back to a specific day and
know for sure. In the same way, we need to be able to look back
with certainty to the moment when we became Christ's. It doesn't
just happen. It is a transaction between us. It is a conscious and intentional act. Can you look back to that moment? If not, let it be
now. With a simple prayer, our lives are redeemed by God. And are

you ready for the delicious surprise of all that it means to be redeemed? Chew on this!

> *to buy back*
> *to free from what distresses or harms us*
> *to free from captivity by payment of ransom*
> *to extricate from or help to overcome something*
>   *detrimental*
> *to release from blame or debt*
> *to clear*
> *to free from the consequences of sin*
> *to change for the better!*
> *to reform, repair, restore, rescue, retrieve*
> *to remove the obligation of*
> *to exchange for something of value*
> *to fulfill*
> *to make good!*
> *to make worthwhile*
> *to offset or compensate for a defect*
> *to extinguish guilt incurred by*
> *to make amends for*

Rich with you in Christ,
Laura

Lord Jesus, thank You for Your obedience to the Father. It secured our forgiveness. May we live obedient lives worthy of the name we took when we became Yours—Christian. Amen.

I call on you, O God, for you will answer me

—PSALM 17:6

23 OCTOBER

Dear Friends,

Many times in recent months an unwelcome thought has pushed its way to the surface during my prayer time. "Do you really believe this makes a difference?" I ignore it, a taunt from the enemy. Then another, "Why do you pray?" I have found these questions scrawled on old church bulletins and in the pages of my prayer journal. Both have recurred often enough that I have had to stop and consider them. I no longer dismiss them as challenges from the enemy. In fact, I recognize them now as necessary and legitimate questions that God is urging me to answer for myself. We can, perhaps, only go so far with Him in prayer until we do.

Recent experience has thrust these questions back into the forefront of my thinking. There will be no more putting them off. And what recent experience is forcing me to consider my beliefs about prayer? The answers to prayer that have come! I have a prayer list started last June comprising four months of concerns and requests. Looking over it, I am astonished at the answers I have had. One after another. One more unlikely than the next.

The list delights me surely, and has increased my faith in God and in prayer. But that record of answered prayers also surprises me. And that surprise is what has stopped me in my tracks. Why am I surprised? Don't I pray expecting Him to answer? Not always. In fact, many of those circumstances were ones I doubted would improve. I approached God about them with resignation and doubt.

But this has given rise to a great realization and an important truth about prayer—our doubts do not interfere with God's work in a situation. Our hesitant, pessimistic prayers are no less likely to be heard and answered than those prayers offered with a sure, unwavering hand, confident about Who He is. It is not the size of our faith that presses God into action, it is simply the asking. One nod to Him and He is off and running. He is only waiting to be asked, and prayer is the invitation.

Sometimes we will pray doubting. But doubt is not to be confused with unbelief. Hallesby makes that distinction in his great book *Prayer* (pp. 31-35) Unbelief is an act of the will, it is a refusal to trust God. We believe. Our coming to God in prayer demonstrates that belief. Doubts sometimes come because we are fallible and human. But those doubts do not nullify our prayers. He hears us because we trust Him, because in our need we turn to Him.

Every time God challenges me to articulate my personal understanding of prayer He is demanding that I consider this: "Who do you think I am?" "When you come to Me in prayer, do not come trusting in your own eloquence or fervor or degree of faith but in Who I am."

Here we are back where we always end up—at our need to get to know Him better. Time alone with Him is always what He is calling us to and leading us to. The better we know Him the less we will be surprised by unlikely answers to prayer. And the more we will dare in prayer. Nothing more accurately reflects our understanding of God than our prayer lives do. And prayer itself is exactly where our understanding of Him will grow and deepen and catch fire.

In Christ,
Laura

Father God, Lead me in prayer. Show me Your glory. Amen.

. . . regard us as servants of Christ and as those entrusted
with the secret things of God.

— 1 CORINTHIANS 4:1

30 OCTOBER

Dear Friends,

My favorite Bible passage on prayer is the one in Exodus 33 when Moses goes out from the camp to meet with the Lord. As he makes his way out to the Tent of Meeting, all the Israelites stand to their feet in reverence. Once in the tent, "the Lord would speak with Moses . . . as a man speaks with his friend."

As well as I know that passage, I noted something today in the wording that amused me. You will notice the Lord spoke with Moses "as a man speaks with his friend" not as a woman speaks with her friend. I'm glad of that. Friends and I often are so delighted to be together again that we tend to jump right into conversation before the key is even out of the ignition, and the jabbering doesn't end till we drive away. We laugh and interrupt each other and leap from topic to topic barely taking the time to note our surroundings or take a breath. Only when I get home do I realize how many threads of conversation were left dangling. I'm sometimes exhilarated but frustrated by how short the time was and by our rapid-fire updates that don't always do justice to the important concerns of our lives. I may also regret something I said, or remember too late what I failed to mention but had intended to.

Such concerns need not come up in our prayer conversation. The Lord graciously offers us the continuous opportunity to apologize, to clear up misspoken words and to say all that we want to. We literally have all the time in the world to get everything said and need never fear our time with the Lord running out. That in itself calms our conversation.

I had lunch with a friend recently whom I don't see often. We had scheduled it weeks in advance as we always do, and I looked forward to it as usual. But as the day approached chores closed in and I thought seriously about canceling. We can catch up almost any time, and I had numerous tasks to attend to before leaving on a trip the next day. But in the end I went, and how grateful I am that I did. It turned out that my friend had been anticipating our time together with great urgency because she had something important to convey. There is an area of deep concern regarding one of her children and she wants me to be praying with her about the situation.

The experience was an important lesson for me. We come to prayer with desires and areas of concern. But God does too. He has a plan for our prayer time. He comes to it with an agenda of His own. So when we put off praying, when we delay or decide we have no real need of it today, or time for it, we ignore the most important considerations: What does the Lord have to say to me today? What would He share with me? What new way is He planning today to tell me that I am cherished? Where does He want to send me today as His loving hands and feet? What or whom does He want to entrust to me today to pray over with Him?

Our prayer time is a conversation with One who anticipates it more eagerly than we do. He knows perfectly all that it will yield and how much depends upon our showing up.

And here you sit, reading. Go! Our Friend is waiting!

> with you in Him,
> Laura

Loved Lord, Thank You for reminding me that my prayer time is Yours, too. Take it and make of it what You will. May I think of it rightly. May I approach it with reverence because You are there, and with excitement because You want me there with You. In Christ, Amen.

Now about brotherly love we do not need to write to you,
for you yourselves have been taught by God to love each other.

— I THESSALONIANS 4:9

6 NOVEMBER

Dear Friends,

A deepening understanding of Who God is and of who we are as His loved children will best grow in that quiet, focused time that we intentionally set aside each day for prayer. That will also be the time we most clearly will hear His voice to us of reassurance, of correction, conviction and direction. Committing to such a quiet time not only signals our willingness to hear what He would say to us, but also a willingness to consider what we hear and to respond rightly to it.

But the daily time set aside for prayer represents only one part of the prayer conversation. When our quiet time ends and we take up the tasks of the day, prayer is not suspended, it merely shifts into another key. As we go about our errands and work and pleasures, our ongoing conversation with God runs concurrent to the day's activities. We chatter to Him more or less, depending upon our involvements. One sort of prayer is no better or worse than another, only a different flavor. Each is necessary and serves in its way. A close time of honest sharing with a trusting child is only one part of a relationship that is also enriched and enlivened by hasty, happy updates or by calls for assistance or advice.

Last Wednesday I thought throughout the day about something I had read the night before—that all around us are people with needs, that everything we see as we go about our day should give rise to prayer. As I rode a train in Boston, a young man boarded who was obese. He looked around, seemingly hesitant to sit, and I shifted to indicate there was space beside me, and he sat down. Looking up, I saw the couple across the aisle shaking their heads at the boy with looks of disgust, almost hatred. I sat in that noisy, crowded train wanting desperately for this man to know how dearly he is loved by God. And I asked God to tell him. I prayed for him.

An hour earlier, at a lovely small museum, I had walked though its rooms with one of the few other visitors who was there, a woman just my age. She is not someone I've ever met, but I know enough of what we have in common that I prayed for her as we walked along. I don't remember what Caroline Kennedy Schlossberg was wearing that day, but I remember the ways that I asked God to comfort her, to provide for her, to make Himself known to her.

The people all around us, known and unknown, are carried into God's presence by our prayers. Waiting in line, waiting in traffic, daydreaming, people watching—spiritually unfruitful time can be transformed by prayer into something loving and lasting.

Love,

Laura

Father, open my eyes and heart today to whatever You would have me commit to You. More and more, may prayer be my response to whatever I encounter in my day. For Your glory. Amen.

"Can a mother forget the baby at her breast and have no
compassion on the child she has borne? Though she
may forget, I will not forget you! See, I have engraved you
on the palms of my hands . . ."declares the Lord.

—ISAIAH 49:15-18

13 NOVEMBER

Dear Friends,

After church today my husband and I went to our local soup and salad place as we usually do. It's not fancy, not the place for a nice date or special occasion, but it's long been the family favorite for our midday Sunday meal.

In the course of our lunch today it became apparent that something special was going on at the table beside us. The table was so close to ours that it was impossible not to overhear the conversation of the teen-aged girl and woman who were sitting there. Photos were being shared and relationships explained, and before long we realized that this was a meeting of a birth mother and the child she had perhaps not seen since infancy.

This had to be a reunion that had been greatly anticipated by both of them and yet, as I passed them to get some soup, I was surprised to notice that both were wearing torn or dirty jeans and t-shirts. Neither seemed to have put much thought into their appearance. As the meal went on I was startled and saddened by the tales the mother was choosing to share of her high school days and the parties and the boyfriends and what she seemed to think were hilarious adventures. I couldn't see the face of the girl. I wondered what she was thinking.

In such a situation, for such a reunion I would want to put forth my best self, wouldn't you? I would want the meeting to take place somewhere special. I would put thought and time into what I would wear and how I would look and what I would say.

And I thought, of course, of our meetings with God in prayer. I thought of how eagerly He waits for them and how casually we slide into place, if we show up at all. I thought of what a miracle it is that we have been found by and reunited with the One who created us and loves us and spends our entire lifetime longing for us and hoping we will make our way back to Him. And when we do, if we do, after the initial thrill of it, we often forget who it is we are with. We gradually forget what a momentous meeting it is every single time we come to Him to sit or kneel or stand in His presence. We think of it as an inconvenience or an interruption of our more important activities. We rush in and hang around only long enough to hand over our list of demands.

And yet if we would only listen, the things He has to relay to us of who we are, of Who He is, of our heritage and of what is to come! The family pictures He would open to us! Ask Him in prayer to remind you of what you have come from, who you were, all that He has saved you out of. Ask Him to repeat all those promises of what is ahead for us as His. *For I know the plans I have for you, declares the LORD, plans to prosper you and not to harm you, plans to give you hope and a future.* (Jeremiah 29:11).

> your long-lost sister,
> Laura

Father, our true Father, thank You for waiting for us to arrive. Thank You for choosing the very best place and the perfect time and for the feast we have yet to look forward to. We are Yours and You are ours and, like Augustine, we declare that our hearts are restless until we find our rest in Thee. Amen.

Then Haggai, the LORD's messenger, gave this message of the
LORD to the people: "I am with you," declares the LORD.

—HAGGAI 1:13

20 NOVEMBER

Dear Friends,

Looking in a bedside drawer this week I came across an old photo
of me with my brothers Nick and Toby. We are all at breakfast and
smiling happily, Toby in particular. It is his wedding day, July 18,
1987. The date on the back caught my eye because on July 18 of this
year the three of us were also together. That was the day Toby's
bone marrow was transplanted into Nick.

During the six-hour collection procedure Toby wasn't allowed
visitors but I was able to peek in on him once, briefly. Just long
enough for me to feel thoroughly helpless and to note how uncomfortable he was. I went from there to Nick's room at the other end
of the hospital where he was being prepared. There was much coming and going by staff members, and he was agitated and feeling
sick. Not a good time for visitors.

I headed outside to walk and wait. I turned on my cell phone to
update my husband and found a message from my friend and
neighbor, Cindy.

"Hi, Laura. It's me. It's Tuesday about 11:38 and I just want you
to know I'm praying for you and for Nick and Toby and just praising God that He's allowed this procedure to go forward. And that it
will be healing . . . Bye. Love you."

I remember exactly where I was standing in the hot parking lot
as I listened to that message and how it made me cry with gratitude.
I remember the relief I felt knowing that, far from home though we
were, somebody out there was thinking of us and praying for us.

I replayed that message several times, and eventually even copied it down in my prayer journal. It meant that much to me. I also

wanted to save it as a model of what to offer to others in need. Last July 18th, for me, it contained all that a hurting heart needed to hear. With nothing false or extraneous or burdensome, it conveyed all the essentials:

You are not forgotten.

I am praying for you.

God is involved in what you're going through.

I love you.

We can and ought to be praying for one another. And that blessing is broadened when we let our loved ones know not only that we are, but specifically how we are, praying. It takes so few words, too, to lift a friend's eyes to God and to remind them Who He is and that He has everything entirely, eternally, in hand.

> Rich with you in His love,
> Laura

You are 'the LORD who has compassion on me', one of my favorite names for You in the Bible. Thank You. Thank You for the word of comfort and love that You send at the moment it's most needed. Thank You for hearts like Cindy's willing to be Your messenger, for the friends You bless us with, for the opportunities You give us to be a blessing. Father, we are so thankful.

In Christ's name. Amen.

Now you are the body of Christ, and each one of you is a part of it.

— 1 CORINTHIANS 12:27

27 NOVEMBER

Dear Friends,

One of my favorite parts of our Community Bible Study class are the few minutes of prayer the leaders have together before the class day begins. We stand in a circle in one of the classrooms, holding hands, heads bowed and eyes closed. It is usually a smallish circle. I stand holding a loved one's hand, let's say Devon's, and we all pray for one another. Every so often my hand is let go as a latecomer arrives and is taken up again then and the prayers continue. A few minutes later, when we open our eyes, our circle has expanded greatly and Devon is now some distance away, though still connected to me by the chain of joined hands.

That circle always has struck me as a wonderful picture of how God works in our lives. He sends loved ones to take our hands and to pray for us and with us. In time, another friend arrives and we take their hand too, and on it goes. All are linked by prayer, though we may find ourselves, over time, at some physical distance from one or another.

The other night I was rereading old Christmas cards (1994!) and rediscovered one from my friend Priscilla and read a remarkable story of hands separated by physical distance but joined by God. She wrote to me:

"One of my friends in Des Moines has been at the hospital with her dad a lot. He has leukemia. Her parents live in a small town. Her mom stays at Barb's while her dad is in the hospital. About a week ago I dreamed Barb called me and couldn't talk because her dad had died. When I woke up, I prayed for her. Once I got to work, I found out he'd had a very bad night. Thursday, when Barb and I talked, she told me she couldn't pray and so had said my name to God in hopes I'd pray."

I suspect we often fail to recognize what are actually prompts of the Holy Spirit. Why not count every thought of someone that pops into your mind as a call to pray for that person? Even if you're mistaken there would be no loss and great gain.

God is not limited by distance. Near or far, we are connected to our loved ones and usable by God in their lives. If we are near to Him and He is near to them, they are only a prayer away.

> Joined with Him, joined
> with you, Laura

Holy One, lead me in prayer. Use me in the lives of those whose hands are still within immediate reach and those whose hands are not. Call me to pray for those I love and those whom it is hard for me to love. I praise You as omnipresent and unfailingly loving, the Lord who provides. And Father, bless those who, in obedience to You, pray for me. Amen.

He put a new song in my mouth, a hymn of praise to our God.

— PSALM 40:3

4 DECEMBER

Dear Friends,

A few years ago on an April day I drove up to Santa Monica for my cousin Rena's birthday party. Her little house was packed with friends and loved ones, most of whom I had never met. A lot of delicious things were happening in every direction as I came in— two cakes were being decorated and strawberries cleaned. A big pot of beans on the stove had been bubbling for hours and a pan of chicken was marinating in lime juice and garlic and wonderful-smelling spices. There were gifts piled up and bunches of flowers inside and out. As more friends arrived they spilled out of the house and into the backyard where we talked and laughed sitting at scattered picnic tables under strings of little white lights. The grill was heating and Cuban jazz was playing and kids were running every which way and this party was happening!

As the afternoon turned into evening, the laughter continued and the conversation deepened and good food just kept coming out of that tiny kitchen. If you paid attention you would have noticed little snatches of humming here and there, in the house and outside. Something great was about to happen and we waited.

Rena's friend Carla, a songwriter, had written a birthday song for Rena. All afternoon, one guest at a time, she had taken us aside and taken us into her confidence and had taught us, in whispers, her song.

When the flower-covered cakes were brought out from the kitchen, Rena was surrounded by her parents and friends and husband and children and loved ones. And all of us—strangers though many of us had been until that day—began to sing, in perfect unison, the love song for Rena.

I wish you could have heard us. I wish you could have seen Rena's face. I wish you could have seen Carla's face. She had never heard her song sung by any voice but her own.

We avoid prayer. We dread it. We resent it as assigned work or obligation. But do you see what God is calling each of us to in daily quiet time? He's calling us away from the party for a moment with Him alone. He's beckoning with a smile. He has a surprise and it is gorgeous. He wants to teach us His song.

And when we go back out about our day we'll hear snatches of it in the most unlikely places. And with people we might never have expected, we will find ourselves singing. And all those with whom we most want to be singing but are not yet, we can whisper their names to Him while we are learning His song. He's calling to them, too. He is everywhere inside the house and out in the yard, calling to each one. And the very thing that will cause them to lift their heads and to rise to follow Him will be the sound of our singing.

With you in Him,
Laura

Thank You for calling us to prayer. Thank You for how eagerly You anticipate our meeting with You in that secret place. Thank You for how dearly You love the sound of our voices laughing and talking and singing. More and more may we see prayer as You do. And may we run to join You there. In Christ. Amen.

The Lord will save me and we will sing . . .

—ISAIAH 38:20

II DECEMBER

Dear Friends,

There is a line in a commentary I read years ago that I have never forgotten: "Since unbelief is, at heart, a moral rather than an intellectual problem, no amount of evidences will ever turn unbelief to faith. But the revealed Word of God has the inherent power to do so."

Faith is not based on sight. A decision to believe is made even in the absence of certain knowledge. God has spoken in the Bible. We choose to believe that Christ is who He says He is, or we do not.

In his autobiography, Billy Graham talks about a decisive moment in his life when he was a young man and already a believer. He had accepted Christ's forgiveness years before. But this night was a turning point for him in another area. This was the night he held his Bible in his hand and said to God, "Lord, there is much in this Bible that I don't understand and there is a lot I can't explain. And there is a lot I can't even believe in my natural mind. But I believe You. And You say this is Your divinely inspired Word. And You say it is true. So tonight I say to You, I accept this entirely as Your Word." He made a decision.

And what followed for Graham? What follows any decision to take God at His Word? God rewards our belief with confirmation and certain knowledge. He pours in with one confirmation after another. The proofs come, but they come after we believe, not before. Proof does not inspire our belief, it rewards it. Jesus performed miracles not to convince unbelievers to believe. His miracles rewarded those who already believed and came to Him trusting in what He could do for them.

It is the same with God's love. God loves you personally. Deeply.

Truly. His Word says He does. Do you doubt it? Are you waiting for additional proof? He allowed His Son to die for you. Would you ask for more? Have you, like me, spent years trying to feel God's love? Have you tried and failed to believe it in your natural mind? Accepting God's love requires that we take Him at His Word. We can say as Billy Graham did, "I can't even believe it in my natural mind. But I believe You."

Once we do, once we go to God and say, "I believe You love me. I accept Your Word. I'm sorry it took so long. Thank You that You love me," confirmations follow. A sure sense of His love is poured out. And, secure in God's love, we are freed. We can cease our striving. We are fed. We become available to others in a new way. And our prayer time comes to life.

My understanding of prayer, my love for it, my commitment to it, are entirely different than they were a year ago. And not from learning a prayer method or reading a good book or making a vow or changing my attitude or committing to pray so many minutes a day. My prayer life has been transformed by a simple decision. God tells me that He loves me. And I have decided to believe Him.

Loved,

Laura

Thank You for Your presence with me. Thank You for Your love for me. You hear this from me all the time, don't You? I will say it forever. Amen.

If we confess our sins, He is faithful and just to forgive us
our sins and to cleanse us from all unrighteousness.

— 1 JOHN 1:9

18 DECEMBER

Dear Friends,

Not long ago, I sat down at my computer to work on a prayer letter, but I didn't get very far. A little voice started needling me. "This house really needs to be cleaned..." Now, don't worry. I've heard this voice before. It's persistent, but I know how to handle it. I've had loads of experience. I ignore it.

"Laura, this house really needs cleaning...And the bathrooms really need cleaning!" I ignored it harder. Back to work.

"Lauurraa....."

OK. Concentration officially shot. I knew I'd get nowhere with the letter as long as housecleaning thoughts were driving away prayer letter thoughts. So I gave in; I went downstairs and gathered my mop and cleaning supplies.

In our bathroom I was using something new. This was something the label called a "daily shower cleaner". I sprayed and I rubbed. I sprayed some more. I rubbed harder. Nothing much seemed to be happening. I knew it had been a while, but had I entirely forgotten how to clean a shower? I checked the directions to see if I had missed a step. And what do you think I read?

"For best results, start with a clean shower." For best results, start with a clean shower? This was shower cleaner!

"If starting with a partially soiled shower you will not see immediate results for 2 to 4 weeks." Two to four weeks! This was a daily cleaning product. I had to do this every day for fourteen to twenty-eight days before my shower would be clean?!

Is this how we tend to think of prayer? For best results, start with a clean conscience. A clean soul. A clean slate. Don't come to

God if you are slightly soiled. And if you do decide to slink in guiltily just know that forgiveness may take as long as 2-4 weeks.

I have a friend who refused to take Communion for quite a while. "I'm not worthy," he kept saying, with real regret. Finally his daughter said to him one day, "Dad, of course you're not worthy. That's the point. That's what makes His sacrifice so amazing. And He did it to make communion with you possible. Don't waste it!"

Nothing makes us more hesitant to go to prayer than knowing we have not been who we should have been. We hesitate because we have something to confess. We avoid prayer because we aren't clean. And yet prayer is the very place and way we will be cleansed. And instantly! In the welcome and warmth of His grace we come clean and are forgiven.

Grab your towel and make your way to the showers—the showers of relief, of reconnection and restoration.

Happy almost-Christmas week!
Laura

Father, for the fresh start continually available to us, thank You. May we run to confess without hesitation or fear. For making the way of forgiveness through Christ, thank You. For the gift of Him, we thank You. Amen.

Then Jesus told his disciples a parable to show them
that they should always pray and not give up.

— L UKE 18:1

8 J ANUARY

Dear Friends,

One of my special possessions is a scrap of paper not much bigger
than the paper in a fortune cookie. On it is a prayer written by my
friend Meg. She used to put brief prayers in a small prayer box she
kept.

Meg and I were close friends for over a decade. We shared interests and had long satisfying conversations about faith and life. She
joined our family for several holidays and family celebrations and
talked me through challenges. But Meg was intensely introverted.
She was such a private person that she seemed to find close friendships a bit unnerving at times. Occasionally and without warning,
contact would cease and she would drop out of sight into periods of
solitude. Weeks could go by with no contact.

It was frustrating to say the least. None of her friends were ever
quite sure how to respond. Should we call or not? Better to back off
or keep at it? This was before emails, so it was phone (never answered) or notes in the mail. I have to admit it was tempting to just
let it go. It sometimes felt like too much effort to keep the friendship going. But I missed her. And I knew how rich it could be, and
important for us both. So, without encouragement and despite the
silence, I persisted. I left messages until she responded and contact
resumed.

After Meg died of cancer a few years ago, her mother gave me a
few mementos including several papers from her prayer box that
mentioned my name. And this is my favorite: "When I resisted,
Lord, You still provided friends in Laura and others who would not
give up on me, despite my efforts to pull away. Thank you!"

How grateful I am that I persisted! And so grateful to God for His letting me know that it made a difference. This has been a lasting reminder for me of the importance of persistence even in the face of silence.

Persistent prayer is prayer that continues over weeks and months and years despite apparent silence. With no evidence in sight of it making a bit of difference, this is prayer that continues. It focuses neither on the problem nor the silence but on the answer to come. It focuses on the One by whom that answer will come. Persistent pray-ers keep an eye on the horizon watching for their answer. Their trust is in God, in who He is.

God's silence reflects neither inactivity, absence of caring or deafness. If there is a matter you have prayed and prayed about, persist in prayer. Don't give up. Don't be scared off by the silence. Trust Him. Even as we wait, He is at work; He is accomplishing something. And it is holy and it is good. And it may be in you.

Author Wesley Duewel says, "Prayers prayed in the will of God are never lost but are stored until God gives the answer." Hang on to everything you know about who He is. Trust that His answer will come and that it will be perfectly timed. This is the very definition of faith—being sure of what we hope for and certain of what we do not (yet!) see. (Hebrews 11:1)

Trusting with you,
Laura

Father, Thank You for all You are doing that I do not yet know. Keep my eyes on You. May I persist in prayer, in trust, in You. For Your glory and that Your will may be done. Amen.

Jesus replied, "If anyone loves me, he will obey my teaching.
My Father will love him, and we will come to him
and make our home with him."

— JOHN 14:23

15 JANUARY

Dear Friends,

One of the first chapter books I remember reading by myself and being completely captivated by was *Helen Keller's Teacher.* I was in the third grade, and that book triggered my enduring interest in both Helen Keller and Annie Sullivan.

Last November, driving out of Boston, I squealed at the sight of a large sign: "Perkins Institute for the Blind."

"That's where Annie Sullivan went to school when she was a little girl! Over a hundred years ago." I told my husband excitedly. "She took Helen Keller there to study, too."

A few days later, walking through an exhibit of American treasures at the Library of Congress, I was deeply moved to see a telegram sent by Helen Keller to Alexander Graham Bell. "I need you. I am to speak at meeting for blind Waldorf Astoria New York... Teacher has bad cold and cannot speak. Will you stand beside me and repeat my speech so that all may hear..."

Helen Keller was an adult at the time that telegram was sent in 1907. But, I noted, Annie Sullivan remained "Teacher." Through nearly fifty years of friendship and companionship, in honor of the essential, life-giving role Annie Sullivan had first played in her life, Helen Keller only ever referred to her friend as "Teacher."

As Mary Magdalene wept at the empty tomb she saw a man who asked her, Woman, why are you crying?" Thinking he was the gardener, she asked where Jesus' body had been taken. The "gardener" responded with one word: "Mary!" and she knew Him at once. Her response?

"Teacher!"

Of all the names that could have sprung from her heart to her lips at that moment, what came was, "Teacher."

At the first encounter between the apostles and Jesus, their first recorded word to Him was 'Teacher.' "Teacher, where are you staying?"

When Nicodemus came to Jesus in the night, he said, *"we know you are a teacher who has come from God."*

By what title do you most often address God? Almighty God? Father? Lord? You likely use one or two names over and over when you pray.

I challenge you to try something with me. For the next few days, address all your prayers to Him as "Teacher" and see what it does to your praying. He is as much teacher to us as to His apostles or long-ago followers. Acknowledge Him as such. What has resulted for me has been a fresh appreciation and new awareness of Him in a role in our lives that we don't normally recognize or assign to Him or articulate. Addressing Him by that little-used title makes it impossible to pray on autopilot as we sometimes tend to do. And it forces us to think in a new way about our relationship. That's a guarantee of growth and fresh insight.

In Him,

Laura

Teacher, Thank You for all the life lessons by which You are making us more truly Yours. Thank You that You are right with us in this, and are not barking orders from afar. Amen.

My soul thirsts for God, for the living God.
When can I go and meet with God?

—PSALM 42:2

22 JANUARY

Dear Friends,

In my last semester of college, among other classes I was taking
Spanish and I was taking Greek. I was in that last semester of Spanish because it fulfilled a graduation requirement. But I was in Greek
because I wanted to be. My husband is from Greece and I wanted to
learn his language. I loved him and I wanted to know him better, to
be able to enter more fully into his world and culture. To better
know and experience his country. I wanted to be able to understand
the family stories his mother was always telling.

I went to Spanish class and I did my work faithfully. By one
measure I was a success—I got an A for the semester. But there was
no joy in it. I was there to fulfill a requirement.

Greek was something else. I was there out of love and I worked
hard. Every word I learned excited me as it expanded my ability to
communicate with my husband and his family and to know them.
I never had to force myself to do my homework or to study for a
Greek exam. I studied with my husband's arm around me or his
hand in mine. My progress delighted him.

At the time I didn't seem to be doing as well in Greek as I did
in Spanish—I got better grades in Spanish. No one listening in on
my Greek class would have been dazzled by my grammar or the
smoothness of my delivery. But I never missed a class because I was
there by choice. Love was my motive and love was my reward.

Twenty-five years later I couldn't tell you my Spanish teacher's
name. She had dark hair and was pretty skinny. I remember very
little of her language and culture. But if ever you need help order-
ing an octopus dinner in Greek, I'm your girl. I can ask for a taxi or

say my prayers. I can sit with a lonely Greek woman who wants to tell someone her memories and dreams.

Is prayer for you Greek class or Spanish? How often we think of prayer as a graduation requirement. We may show up faithfully and look and sound adept but have no joy in it. If ever we hear ourselves saying, "I really ought to pray more…" we can know it has become duty. We have forgotten the gift of it and all that it offers.

Prayer is the place to run to. It is not required, it is given; it is offered to us in love. There need be no hesitation or wrestling with it. When our desire is to be with God and to know Him, we have prayer. Drawn by love not dread, we can go easily and often. Don't be slowed by regrets or guilt. Don't let anything keep you from the place that has been prepared for you.

Love awaits!

In Him,
Laura

Loving Lord, thank You for the gift of this. For the welcome when we come. For the open arms. For the relief of it. For the peace in Your presence, the answers and leading, thank You. In Jesus' name. Amen.

Sow for yourselves righteousness, reap the fruit of
unfailing love . . . for it is time to seek the Lord.

—HOSEA 10:12

29 JANUARY

Dear Friends,

I was cleaning the house one day last fall somewhat resentfully. As I yanked the vacuum along behind me, I was grumbling to myself: "I'm an educated woman! I have important things to do. This is a waste of my gifts. Why can't someone else do this? Maybe someone who can't do anything else. And what I really hate is that even if I spend a chunk of time at it, a few days later it needs to be done all over again! It never ends!" And the Lord seemed to nudge me and say: "And that's just how you sometimes think of prayer, too" . . .

I have headed to prayer time with just these thoughts: I don't have time for this! I have important things to do. I need to get going this morning. I have places to be. This is a waste of my gifts. This is a waste of my education. Why can't somebody else do it? Somebody who can't do anything else. And what I really hate is that even if I spend a chunk of time at it, a few days later it needs to be done all over again! It never ends!

What a snob I have often been about prayer. Is prayer only for old ladies and clergy? For those without any real gifts? Is it only for the super-spiritual or those without a social life? Is prayer the menial labor of Christianity? Am I too valuable to God to waste my time praying? Maybe I'd be better used elsewhere—probably somewhere more visible . . .

S.D. Gordon, in his great book *Quiet Talks on Prayer,* first published 101 years ago, says this: "The great people of the earth today are the people who pray. I do not mean those who talk about prayer; nor those who say they believe in prayer; nor yet those who can explain about prayer; but I mean these people who take time and pray.

They have not time. It must be taken from something else. This something else is important. Very important, and pressing, but still less important and less pressing than prayer. There are people that put prayer first, and group the other items in life's schedule around and after prayer . . .

"It is wholly a secret service. We do not know who these people are, though sometimes shrewd guesses may be made. I often think sometimes we pass some . . . woman . . . and hardly give her a passing thought, and do not know, nor guess, that perhaps she is the one who is doing far more for her church, and for the world, and for God than a hundred who would claim more attention and thought, because she prays; truly prays as the Spirit of God inspires and guides."

We so often wear ourselves out doing more than God has asked us to do. We forget that what He does is what matters, and our part is to invite Him in. Our part is to step out of the way and watch Him work. Our part is to cheerfully cheer all that He does, all that He sets right and fixes and comforts and mends and clarifies in answer to prayer.

Our part is to pray. And our prayers open the door and allow entrance to the King of Kings. There is nothing menial about that. Those privileged to open the door to Him by prayer can be the first to see Him enter in. And when He does, our hearts can be the first to applaud His entrance and to rejoice in all that it promises.

With you at the door,
Laura

Lead us, Father. May we be faithful to invite You in to every situation and every life that You are poised and eager to pour into. May we do our part so that You can do Yours. Thank You for this privilege, this co-labor. In Christ, Amen.

... humbly accept the word planted in you ...

—JAMES 1:21

5 FEBRUARY

Dear Friends,

There is an image that has stayed with me for weeks. Last November I stood alongside a woman and watched as she prepared her vegetable garden for winter. Last summer's plants were long gone, and she was clearing away dried stalks and old leaves. Here and there against the dark soil I could see the yellow of a squash or other colorful vegetable.

"Those will be plowed under," she told me. "We leave them there on purpose. They will be turned under and will enrich the soil for next year's crop."

Here was bright, whole, perfectly formed fruit that would never see the light of day, would never rest on a table or feed a hungry body. And yet it was right where it was needed. It would serve in exactly the place and manner for which it was intended—to improve the soil out of which it had grown.

It brought to mind God's work in each of us, the fruit He is producing in our lives. We feed so richly on all that comes to us from Him. When the reassurance or direction we receive so exactly meet our immediate need, we delight in telling others about those perfect answers.

But not everything the Lord shares with us in prayer and study is intended for others. Some of it is for us alone - personal, private blessing that will remain between us and God. Its presence, though, enriches us and will produce a richer crop of what will be shared. The food between just the two of us is as valuable and nourishing as the food that is shared, but it is secret, private, sacred food.

These are the great gifts—those assurances known to one heart alone. "I know," He seems to say. "I know it all. I know that most private pain. I am here. I can assuage it, and I will." He has the perfect word.

There is much in a relationship between husband and wife that is never shared with others—private exchanges and inside jokes that are known to them alone. But that unseen portion of their life together enriches the soil out of which everything else grows—their parenting, their self images, their effectiveness in the workplace, their friendships. In the same way, our unseen private life with God informs and dictates our more public life. It touches all of our relationships.

While corporate worship and study are vital and necessary, there are things He will entrust to us only when we are alone. And as with any other, the strength and depth of this relationship will be established in private time together. There is fruit He wants to hide in our hearts in quiet today that will, in time, yield so much for so many.

In Christ,

Laura

Heavenly Father, how eagerly You await us in the place of prayer. May we take time apart with You today with hands ready to rest and ears ready to listen and eyes willing to close to all the distractions that seek to divert us or to lure us from Your side. In Christ's name. Amen.

Let us then approach the throne of grace with confidence,
so that we may receive mercy and find grace to
help us in our time of need.

—HEBREWS 4:16

12 FEBRUARY

Dear Friends,

A few years ago, when my son was beginning his college search, the subject was much on all of our minds. At a family wedding, I asked my cousin Tom about his experience at Harvard years ago.

"Of all my friends at Harvard I'm sure I got the best education."

"How did you manage that?"

"Office hours!"

Every professor at every school is required to spend a certain number of hours each week in his or her office and available to students. Tom told me, "Here I was at a school with some of the greatest minds in the world on almost any subject you could think of. And all I had to do was show up on the right day at the designated hour and I could go in and ask questions and hear all about their work and plans. And that's what I did every week, all four years. It was amazing." Tom got what he came for. He knew where to go, and he went.

Queen Esther, the king's own wife, faced possible death for entering his throne room and approaching the king uninvited. But she went because she knew that only there, only from him, would she get the specific help she needed against her enemy Haman. And she did. She got what she came for.

We have immediate, free access to Almighty God, who is our Father. For us, the door is always open. We are limited neither to certain hours nor to a specified number of years. We don't have to wait to be summoned. We face no risk at all in going. And yet we hang back. With no reason to hesitate or fear, we hesitate anyway;

we do fear. We don't believe the door will be open. We don't believe He means it. We don't believe we will find there what we need. We don't believe we will be welcomed. We favor alternatives. We try to manage in our own strength.

Jill Briscoe, a favorite writer of mine, realized too late that when she was in college, on her very campus having weekly office hours, was C.S. Lewis.

We realize too late that on our very campus is Christ Himself. We forget what is available to us every day of our lives. When we're worried, we have forgotten. When we're afraid, we have forgotten. When our hearts sink and we're tempted to despair, we have forgotten. When all the discouraging thoughts break through and we start to believe the lies, we have forgotten.

We are not alone. We have something much greater and more powerful to hope in and rely on and rest against than self-help, will power, stiff upper lip, elbow grease, support groups, positive thinking, or gumption (whatever that is).

We are children of the King. The door is open, His arms are open. Our names are engraved on His heart, on the palms of His hands.

With you in Him,
Laura

Father, Thank You for the free and continual access we have to You through prayer—to Your practical help, Your leading, Your forgiveness. Lend us Your eyes to see in new ways all those things we turn to instead. May we believe Your love and come to You in our need, nowhere else. For Your joy. Amen.

You are not your own; you were bought at a price.

— I CORINTHIANS 6:20

19 FEBRUARY

Dear Friends,

Not long ago we had a young woman to dinner, a graduate student who was in town for several months from her native Spain. She was here doing research with my husband and his colleagues on ocean wave formation. When she shared some photographs with us of her home on a high rocky cliff in northern Spain, it was quickly apparent how she came upon her field of study—her family home is a lighthouse! Her father is a lighthouse keeper. The family moved several times throughout her childhood, each time from one lighthouse to another. She has never lived in any other kind of dwelling. Her father's work has always dictated their home—where and how they lived. Always by the water, of course; always where the lighthouses are.

"I am called to be a lighthouse." I found that line in my prayer journal last night written months ago. Each of us is a lighthouse and out of us shines His beam. We don't have the luxury of moving wherever, whenever. Our Father's work dictates where and how we live. Only He knows where the lost boats are. Only He knows where the endangered ships and seamen and women. He knows who most needs to see His light shine this very day—those without it will crash and drown.

We need to be where He wants to shine from. His light is for them, but also for us. Without it, we know nothing beyond our own shoes, our own shores. Without His light we are empty and dark inside, something just to be looked to and admired on the horizon, only visible in daylight and from close at hand, something to pass by but then dismiss. Without His light we are no use to those in the distance, in the water, those trying to avoid the rocks and threat.

Like me, are you feeling a tug to be somewhere other than where you are? Are you longing to be elsewhere? All week I was wrestling with being here. I wanted to be in Australia with my husband. I wanted to be at the hospital with my brother. I wanted to be hiding out in a dark movie theatre or under the covers. But this week, this is where I was supposed to be. Home. Praying. Waiting. This is where He was working. In me. Preparing me for the week ahead, for a phone call I dread telling me that my brother has died.

We can't know whom He is leading to safety from within us. But we can know to do our part, we can know to pray. We pray that we'll be where He needs us to be. We pray for willing hearts, for more trust. We pray our thanks for His light and, on these rocky cliffs, for our solid footing as His.

His, yours,
Laura

Light of the World, lead our prayers and hear them. May we be willing to be where You need us to be and want us to be. Be with us there. Shine on us and in us and through us and in spite of us. For Your glory. Amen.

"For my thoughts are not your thoughts, neither are your ways my ways," declares the LORD.

"As the heavens are higher than the earth, so are my ways higher than your ways and my thoughts than your thoughts."

—ISAIAH 55:8-9

26 FEBRUARY

"He wants to go out."

"He wants to be fed."

"I'm going to write a prayer letter about the two of us arguing about what the cat is saying!"

"But you're only guessing. I know exactly what he's saying..."

You would laugh at some of the conversations that heat up at our house. I have gone to great lengths to win the most nonsensical debates and have responded ridiculously when I lost. Often I don't even care about whatever I'm insisting upon, but something else is being played out. The flame is fueled by that unspoken, ever-present determination: "This is going to go MY way!"

Each of us faces a battle, and it is a worthy one, to identify and silence that inner prima donna. What a tangle she tends to make of things. Only recently have I realized that I need to guard my prayer life against her as well. She is active in her interference. How often, when a prayer of mine is not answered as I'd hoped, do I feel affronted. "But God, it's me! You know me! You like me! How can this be??"

It is easy to begin to think of prayer as something to win at, something from which we can net some gain. It's even easy to think we are owed.

When we think of prayer only as a means of getting something, we are missing a larger, richer picture. If a prayer isn't answered as I'd hoped and I'm angry or afraid, I may have lost sight of what prayer is and what my part in it is supposed to be. Often my trust is not in God but in myself and my ability to charm or persuade or manipulate or win. But loudness or length of prayers, tone of voice or impressive vocabulary won't push our prayers to the head of the line.

We pray because God Almighty has invited us into conversation with Him. The objective of prayer is prayer, sharing. He asks us to pray, and to pray trusting in His love for us and in His promise to hear. And we need to guard that trust and maintain it, regardless of whatever answer comes. Once we make a request, the matter is His and the outcome is His, just as we are His—all of it safe in His hands, and best left there.

With you in Him,
Laura

Lord, even though it stings, thank You that You show us when we're being ridiculous. And thank You for the graceful way out that's always open to us through prayer. Show us the parts of our lives where we're trusting in something or someone other than You. We ask this for Your honor and in Jesus' Name. Amen.

I am the LORD, the God of Israel, who summons you by name . . .
I summon you by name and bestow on you a title of honor.

—ISAIAH 45:3-4

5 MARCH

Dear Friends,

We spend time considering the many names, titles and descriptions
by which God is known in the Bible, and there are many. I have a
book that lists over three hundred of them.

Have you ever considered His names for you? Those who belong to the Lord, who have accepted His forgiveness, are identified
in many loving ways in the Bible. And each name adds another di-
mension to the rich picture of who we are in God's sight. These are
only some of your names from the book of Isaiah—just one book of
sixty-six!

holy	*the Daughter of Zion*
daughter	*the garden of His delight*
the Holy People	*the Redeemed of the LORD*
Sought After	*Your people*
a royal diadem in the hand of your God	*the vineyard of the LORD Almighty*
the City no Longer Deserted priests of the LORD	*ministers of our God the one who trusts*
the humble	*righteous*
the work of My hands	*His flock lambs*
holy to the LORD	*the living, the living*
My servant, whom I uphold	*My witnesses*
My chosen one in whom delight	*summoned by name; you are mine*

precious

called by My name

the LORD's

My holy ones

*called by the name
of Israel*

you who call on the LORD

My servant

citizens of the Holy city

honored in My sight

whom I have chosen

My people

a people the LORD has blessed

*a crown of splendor in the
LORD's hand*

you are Mine

a planting of the LORD

honored in the eyes of the LORD

*My people, My chosen, the people I formed for Myself that
they may proclaim My praise*

*you whom I have upheld since you were conceived and
have carried since your birth*

you will be called Hephzibah ["my delight is in her"]

*you will be called by a new name that the mouth of
the LORD will bestow*

We call ourselves harried and hurried, tired and tense, but we are His. We call ourselves burdened and cheated and forsaken. We are His. Redeemed, held, led and loved. Chosen, jealously guarded, treasured, hidden in the shadow of His wings. We are His. Saved, restored, gathered to Him, comforted. Fed not forgotten. Rewarded and rested and safe. We are His.

> Eternally, gladly,
> Laura

Father, we are not adrift, but Yours. We are not cast away, but Yours. We are known to You and loved by You and claimed by You. Thank You that our names are in Your Book. Amen.

The precepts of the Lord are right, giving joy to the heart
The commands of the Lord are radiant, giving light to the eyes

— PSALM 19:8

12 MARCH

Dear Friends,

One night last year I was up late reading in my Boston hotel room. When the fire alarm went off, I didn't take it seriously. I know how common false alarms are and that hotels are required to test their systems periodically. After peeking into the empty hallway I decided there was no real danger. It was only after looking out the window a few minutes later and seeing three fire trucks at the hotel entrance 23 floors below that I took the alarm seriously and responded appropriately. I dressed quickly and joined the stream of people in the stairwell making their way down to the lobby and then outside to wait in the street. As it happened the problem was a minor one and we were back to our rooms before long, but I've often thought about my initial disbelief and my foolish hesitation.

There were alarms in my heart this morning. I woke with regrets about things I had said and done in the last couple of days but thankfully, in this case at least, I responded rightly to the warning. I responded to regret as God intends.

Regret is a call not to denial or to self-recrimination but to prayer. We have been given a great promise and gift in confession. We can take anything at all to our Father, and in the strength and safety of His presence can look at it clear-eyed and honestly without offering excuses or justification. What a relief to simply admit all of it, to spell it out and to agree that it is unworthy of Him and of us as His.

Once we do, it is finished. He takes it and it is gone. Forgiven. Anything we confess He promises to remember no more [Hebrews 8:12]. We may or may not feel that forgiveness but we cannot judge by feelings. Feelings are unreliable. God is not. He is unchanging and true. Regardless of how we feel we must take Him at His Word. So after talking to Him today, even before I felt better, I thanked Him for forgiving me. I thanked Him for what I knew He had done. He stands with us; we are not alone. And He stands eager to forgive, eager to forget.

A guilty conscience is a wonderful thing—it is a sign of life. It is evidence of a heart being renewed and cleansed, a heart learning the difference between right and wrong. Regret is evidence of our desire to please God and it is evidence of His Father love for us. It is His assurance to us of how actively He is molding and maturing us, how committed He is to our best. But regret will only benefit us if we respond to it as He intends, if we allow it to drive us to Him.

With you in Christ,
Laura

Father, thank You for how You bless and rescue and relieve us. Thank You that You never look the other way. And that nothing that threatens us passes by You unseen, nothing from within and nothing from without. You know all, You rule over all and we are safe. Thank You for that great truth. In Jesus' name. Amen.

*Dear children, keep away from anything that might
take God's place in your hearts.*

— I JOHN 5:21 (NLT)

19 MARCH

Dear Friends,

I found Marcella in 1997. In the end, I hired one of those search companies. It took them ten days to find someone for whom I had been looking for close to thirty years.

Marcella came to live with us the week my mother died when I was nine. She had red hair and a brisk manner and I liked her instantly. She cooked and cleaned up my brothers and me and took charge of things at home. Late at night I sometimes sneaked into her room to talk things over and to watch her say her prayers. I had never seen a grown up kneeling at a bedside to pray.

It was just before Christmas and I was in the fifth grade when Marcella left. My father had remarried by then and she found other work. I was at school when she left, and none of us ever saw her again.

My search over the years was an informal and sporadic one. I called anyone in the local phonebook who shared her last name, but there were many. I had little else to go on.

Marcella had been my haven and advisor during a formative time of my life, but in the years of her absence she had grown even larger in my mind and heart. When things weren't right or I needed answers or direction, my thoughts often turned to her. Marcella would know what to do. If only I could find Marcella.

In 1997 I hired a search company for $144 and just ten days later an envelope arrived in the mail while I was away at a women's retreat. When I got home on Sunday, there it was—a single sheet of paper containing Marcella's address and telephone number. Should I call? She lived across the country and it was already 9:30 at night her time. Was it too late? She would be in her 70s by now. I had to call. I had waited 29 years and didn't want to wait another minute. I dialed and almost held my breath until a woman answered.

"May I speak to Marcella, please?"

A pause. "Who's calling?"

I gave my name and explained in brief.

"This is Marcella's daughter. I'm here packing up. My mother died two days ago."

Two days. Would the pain have been less sharp if I'd learned she had died years before? Probably. The timing, however, was God's, though it would be a very long, angry time before I would be willing to consider God's hand or purpose in any of these events. But a decade later, today for the first time I considered the timing of Marcella's death in light of the retreat theme of that very weekend— Hosea 10:12, *"It is time to seek the Lord."*

Oswald Chambers wrote, "Our soul's personal history with God is often an account of the death of our heroes." God turned me to Him by the death of my friend. But He also turned me to Him by her life and example. How many nights when I looked to her for answers had I seen her look to God? How often had I watched her kneel to pray?

Allow the children in your life to catch you at prayer.

> with love,
> Laura

Sovereign God, Your timing is perfect even when we doubt it. Your love is unfailing even when we can't believe it. May Your will prevail even against our fearful, pained protests. May our trust in You grow and endure. For Your glory. Amen.

My intercessor is my friend as my eyes pour out tears to God . . .

—Job 16:20

26 March

Dear Friends,

I heard from a loved friend recently that God had spoken to her through something I'd written. The message from Him had been clear and timely, she said, but also a very hard one. I felt almost apologetic at that, and rather than pray for her, my immediate desire was to rescue her, to make her feel better. I wanted to say, "No, wait, I probably wasn't clear. He may not have meant that. You may be seeing something that isn't there. God couldn't have intended anything uncomfortable. Certainly not painful."

But of course at times God does allow pain. He is at work on us and in us actively, mightily, building for Himself a kingdom, making us holy as He is holy. So there are things He will talk to us about. He may be asking that we face painful truths we don't want to hear. He may be asking of us something that frightens us. He may be proposing a painful pruning, a letting go.

My reaction to my friend caused me to think about what it means to be a true friend and how we can best pray for loved ones when the Lord is leading them through something painful. Years ago my friend Carrie's daughter was going through a divorce and someone said to Carrie, "whatever else you pray for your daughter, don't pray her out of this pain." Don't pray her out of this pain. I have never forgotten that admonition. I so much want to pray loved ones (particularly my child) out of pain or difficulty. When I am helpless to make things better or easy or pain-free, I ask and expect God to work in the situation the way I would if I could—take the pain away! I place their comfort above all. But God does not. I have heard it said that God is less concerned with our comfort than our character. He is a much wiser parent than I.

Through my writing God convicted my friend of something painful but necessary. Rather than dread her pain I want rather stand strongly, prayerfully, with her. I want to convey my confidence in her and in Him. I want to thank Him for what He is doing for her and asking of her. I am grateful for her ears to hear Him and her recognition of His hand in this. I want to thank Him for His love for her and His dedication to her sanctification. He wants the best in her and for her, He cares that much. While I am content to let her stay comfortable, He is lovingly calling her to be stretched and matured and filled with greater and greater experiences of Him and of herself as His. I am robbing her by hanging back in fear and worry. He wants to show her a freedom glorious and unimagined.

I want to pray not that her pain be removed, but that she be strengthened to bear it. That the measure of her trust in Him will increase and not be linked in any way to her circumstances. I want to pray that His entire plan for her will be accomplished and that it will result in glory for Him and joy for her. I wish for her all that He lovingly envisions and plans for her. And when He chooses to use me in the sometimes painful work He is doing in someone's life, I want to be thankful rather than apologetic. I will be a truer, more valuable friend when I am willing to abide pain and able to calmly sit in its presence trusting Him.

Learning to Love,
Laura

Heavenly Father, You want the best for us, and insist upon it. Thank You for the quality of that love. Teach us to be such parents and friends. May our trust in You be unshakable and solid and rooted in who we know You to be, not in how things go. In Jesus' name. Amen

Do not let your mouth lead you into sin.

— Ecclesiastes 5:6

2 April

Dear Friends,

The apostle Paul suggests in Philippians 3 that if one's spiritual status was based upon earthly pedigree—tribe, heritage, standing among one's people—he would be all set. My mother's family, the Mavericks, are a tribe loudly proud of their role in Texas history. And although my sense of self is not rooted in the exploits of my ancestors, I must admit that I do take inordinate pride in *gobbledygook*. My great-great uncle Maury Maverick added that word to the English language. He used it to describe the wordy, unintelligible nonsense that flew back and forth in Congress when he was congressman under FDR and mentor to Lyndon Johnson. It is a fine word. In honor of Uncle Maury I probably should have so named my first child. Gobbledygook Georgakakos would have been a standout in any crowd.

"Gobbledygook" is the word that came to mind when I recently read 2 Tim 2:16—*Avoid godless chatter, because those who indulge in it will become more and more ungodly.*

I have always thought godless chatter meant only gossip, but it occurs to me that any talk that does not reflect the truth of who God is can be considered godless chatter. He is unfailingly loving. He is the One who rules in all things, the One who has ordained what is happening in each of our lives right now. So with any expression of dissatisfaction we are saying, "God, You messed up." We are suggesting that He is hard or unloving or mistaken. Complaints could be considered as blasphemous as curses.

What other expressions deny the truth of who God is? Angry words, self-pitying statements, expressions of hopelessness, any comment that is critical of self or others—anything we say that refutes that God is lovingly, actively involved in all that happens may be regarded as godless chatter.

I never noticed until recently that this Timothy verse calls godless chatter an "indulgence," that is, something we yield to. So apparently we have a choice about giving in to it. We can ask Him, then, to overrule our impulses and to guard what comes out of our mouths. We can pray that any words we say will be words that honor Him.

I want to pay attention even to the words I use when I pray. Do they express hope and trust in who He is or fear about the state of things around me? Do they express gratitude in who I know Him unchangingly to be or annoyance that His will is being done, but not always mine? I once heard a teacher I like say this about a family crisis of hers: "I heard myself praying like an unbeliever."

In 1 Peter we are urged to live as aliens and strangers in this world. An important way we can stand out as His is by what we say and what we will not allow ourselves to say. We are to be mavericks, if you will—those who refuse to go along with the crowd. Although family tradition gives *maverick* a more complex history, Webster's maintains that Samuel Maverick, my grandfather's great-grandfather, refused to brand his cattle. So all those that stood out from the herd in this way were known as *Maverick*'s, later *mavericks*. I can think of no better description of how we are expected to handle ourselves as believers—to stand out from the crowd.

God's gal,
Laura

Lord God, Maker of heaven and earth, may every inclination of our hearts and every word of our mouths affirm what we know to be true about You and Your love and grace. Thank You for our heritage as Yours and our future as Yours. Thank You that we are never without You and we never will be. Yeeha! Amen.

There is a time for everything, and a season for every activity
under heaven: . . . a time to be silent and a time to speak . . .

— ECCLESIASTES 3:1,7

9 APRIL

Dear Friends,

As we headed to my cousin Rena's house last Thanksgiving I looked forward to seeing my Uncle David as it had been almost two years since I'd seen him. But he has Alzheimer's and I wondered if he would remember me.

When I stepped into Rena's kitchen and Uncle David saw me, his face lit up in a joyful smile as he reached for me eagerly and wrapped me in a wordless hug that went on and on. Later, after dinner, we sat together for a long time in the living room—the quietest spot in a crowded house—and held hands, silent. Never have we passed a sweeter time of connection and communion. Only now, after words, after a lifetime of visits and talk and sharing, is our great love for one another perfectly eloquent and uncluttered.

On this Easter holiday we are with my husband's family in Greece. On Good Friday I stood in the church understanding little of the liturgy. But I was not alone in this—ancient Greek is a language so different from the modern language that even many of the Greeks around me didn't understand what was being said. It was quickly apparent, though, that at important moments words would be unnecessary.

I found myself choking up as the dead "body of Christ" (an embroidered tapestry) was carried through the packed church. I joined the people around me in throwing handfuls of flowers onto His body as it passed by. From above, purple and yellow and white and pink blossoms cascaded down onto the tapestry from worshippers in the upper balconies. The scents of flowers and incense and the perfumes brought from home filled the air of that neighborhood church as it prepared this body for burial.

Later in the service the mournful mood suddenly lifted in a glorious enactment. Representing the life that was soon to pour out on all of us from Christ's tomb, the priest scooped up armfuls of flowers that had collected on the tapestry and, throwing out his arms, flung blossoms over the congregation. And again. And again. Flowers flew through the air in all directions and rained down on our heads. The joy and beauty and blessing that are ours as His was conveyed clearly and beautifully.

The Lord speaks to the eye, to the heart. He, the great painter of sunsets, is not limited to words in sharing Himself and His love with us. Often wordlessly, He steers and leads and compels us with a kind and creative hand.

We—articulate, verbose, literate, eloquent—are entangled in talk. We need to get past all that. We need not weary ourselves with a strict allegiance to some prayer format or formula. Prayer is this too—the simple relief and pleasure of walking together, sitting together, being together, without words.

Χριστος Ανεστη! Christ is risen!
Laura

May we rest in Your presence and stop trying to get it just right with You in words. May we rest against You, trusting in Your love, trusting in Your love. Amen.

God, the blessed and only Ruler . . .

— 1 TIMOTHY 6:15

16 APRIL

Dear Friends,

This past weekend my husband and I took a trip to the past. Driving hours from Athens, we went to visit his elderly aunt in the village where his parents were born as were the generations of the family before them for hundreds of years. We walked down a lane to the crumbling stone walls of his parents' childhood homes. The two houses are so near to each other that if you stand between the two, as I did, and stretch out your arms, you can almost reach both. My mother-in-law grew up that close to her future husband. They began to "go together," she tells me, when both were fifteen. Next year they will be eighty-five. They have shared nearly seventy years, years that included civil war and WWII, when the village was occupied and they were active together in the Underground.

Back in Athens last night I was thinking about some of the things they and their village suffered. But when we wander in the past it's easy to lose our way. When Joseph's brothers were thinking back to the time when they had plotted to kill him and then had sold him into slavery, Joseph said something remarkable that refocused them spiritually. *You intended to harm me, but God intended it for good to accomplish what is now being done . . .* (Genesis 50:20)

There is no denying that the human intention was evil. But God had an intention in it also, and His overrules—rules over—all human plans. God intended it, and He intended it for good. He is not haphazard or flippant or "making do." He is living and active in all that happens. He is ruling with complete command and mighty plans. He is never making things up as He goes along or passively observing the circumstances or conditions of our lives. He rules. He is intentional. And His intentions can never be other than what He is. Righteous. Honorable. Loving. Wise. Just. Merciful. Compassionate.

God is ruling and He alone is ruling. He is the blessed and only Ruler. When all we see around us is chaos, or we are in pain or confusion, that is when our spiritual eyes have to take over and we must trust in what is unseen. Hope that is seen is no hope at all. (Romans 8:24).

God intended it for good to accomplish what is **now** being done. God was working in the past to accomplish something that is now being done. And He is working now in our lives to accomplish some things in the future for us, for our children, for others. We can trust Him not only with our present and our future, but with our past as well. He rules and He ruled. He was ruling even before we knew enough to call on His name.

He is the God of your past. He ruled there. He was working with intentionality in your past and mine. And we can trust Him there and then as surely as we can trust Him here and now. We can pray about things in the past as confidently and with the same relief as we pray about our present and future. We pray, after all, to Him who was and is and is to come.

Love,

Laura

Heavenly Father, even before I called myself Yours, You called me "Mine". Give me new eyes to see my past. May I see Your hand there. Thank You for Your Word. Amen.

I give them eternal life, and they shall never perish;
no one can snatch them out of my hand.
My Father, who has given them to me, is greater than all;
no one can snatch them out of my Father's hand.

— JOHN 10:28-29

23 APRIL

Dear Friends,

I know those Old Testament verses comparing us to clay and God
to the potter, and I have sung the church songs about it. The analogy, though, never spoke to me in particular. It always brought to
mind my friend Helen's messy studio with its splattered potter's
wheel and hulking kiln and huge black garbage cans heavy with
slabs of gray clay. Shelf upon shelf held sturdy, utilitarian mugs and
squat teapots and thick vases and dishes in various stages of finish.

But I read these lines recently in a little book: "The potter takes
the clay, kneads and works it until it is pliable. Next he forms a vessel. . ."

He takes it and kneads it and works it. Only then can he begin
to form something of it. I had never considered how much goes on
before usefulness becomes even a possibility. I suddenly looked with
new eyes at much of what had gone on in my life. I reconsidered my
years of wrestling, arguing, fighting for the last word first with
brothers, then with husband. It seems He can't even begin to make
something of us until we're ready to lay all that aside. Yieldedness
(and how we resist it!) is the essential prerequisite to anything He
might be planning. After reading those lines in that book, I wrote
this: "It may be that I am only now becoming pliable enough for
Him to begin to form me into a vessel. I took so long to become pliable (teachable, flexible, agreeable, willing, yielded.)"

I am trying to see the hard things in my life as His working me,
working me, making me pliable, usable. And painful as much of it

has been, the great promise, of course, is in the particular set of Hands that are doing the working. In the enclosure of those hands is where we must be. Because as hard as it can be there, any other place is utterly devoid of hope and potential. As my little book points out, "The most skillful potter cannot make a beautiful vessel out of a lump of clay never put in his hands."

Twice this week I have made my way down to our hotel gift shop to look again at the most exquisite porcelain dishes I have ever seen. Photos show the artists twirling tiny strands of clay and weaving them to form the latticed sides of the bowls and their lace-like rims. They are incredibly intricate and lovely. I see God as potter in each colorful, beautiful vessel. I feel such hope at the sight of what skillful, tender hands can form from the dust of the ground.

> with you in Him,
> Laura

Heavenly Father, How You knead me and how I need You. May I see Your hand in all that happens. Or may I trust in it where I cannot see it. You are at work and You are unfailingly loving. May I remember that and believe it and yield to it. May I join You in what You're doing and not stand peevishly aside demanding my way. May I come forth glorious one day as You have long planned. For Your honor and in Jesus' name. Amen.

Three times a day he got down on his knees and
prayed, giving thanks to his God . . .

—DANIEL 6:10

30 APRIL

Dear Friends,

When the wall of Jerusalem was rebuilt after the exile to Babylon, the people of Judah rededicated themselves to God. At the elaborate rededication ceremony Nehemiah assigned two choirs to give thanks. Their task was held in such high estimation that these choirs preceded everyone else in procession, even the officials and priests. (Nehemiah 12)

My eye was caught the other night by 1Chronicles 16:41, which speaks of *"those chosen and designated by name to give thanks to the Lord."* Designated by name! Am I one of those God has chosen and designated by name to give thanks to Him? Are you? It is an assignment of great honor.

To help ourselves distinguish between praise and thanks we say that we praise God for who He is and we thank Him for what He does. But the distinction is not quite as tidy as that. I tend to thank Him for who He is as often as I praise Him for it. The more we learn of who He is the more thankful we become. Even as we are praising God for who He is, we feel thankful for His every attribute and quality and name. Confessing our sins, we are thankful for His forgiveness. Making intercession, how thankful we are for His promise to hear and meet our needs.

Philippians 4:4-6 says that all of us are to present our every request or need to God in prayer with thanksgiving. "Always" and "in everything" rejoicing in who He is, in what we know He can do, in what we trust He is doing even in circumstances that seem to make no sense.

Thanking Him when we least want to is one of those seemingly nonsensical things we are asked to learn to do. Ephesians 5:19-20 says *Sing and make music in your heart to the Lord, always giving thanks to God the Father for everything, in the name of our Lord Jesus Christ.* It takes practice and sometimes gritted teeth to actually thank Him for those things or circumstances we don't want and would never have chosen, but a willingness to do so seems to be a marker of a maturing faith. It reflects trust in Him and whatever He is orchestrating. Thanking Him may also move us along in the process of accepting or tolerating difficulties because we are acknowledging the reasoning, loving Mind behind what is happening. It also reminds us that we are not alone.

Before feeding the multitudes, Jesus took the loaves and fishes and gave thanks and broke the loaves (Matthew 14:19). At the Last Supper, before giving them to the disciples, He took the cup and the bread and gave thanks (Luke 22). Over and over throughout the Bible the act of giving thanks precedes amazing demonstrations of God's power.

This is a head-lifting, heart-lifting discipline we are asked to master. In changing times it focuses us on unchanging Truth. Giving thanks leads us home every time to who He is, and that's where our hearts, anxious for nothing, can truly rest. (Philippians 4:6)

Thankful with you,
thankful for you, Laura

Thank You, Lord, for who You are and for who I am as Yours. You are worthy of my trust. More and more may I have a thankful heart. May I be faithful in all You have chosen and designated me by name to do. For Your honor and glory. Amen.

Finally, brothers, whatever is true, whatever is noble, whatever is right, whatever is pure, whatever is lovely, whatever is admirable—if anything is excellent or praiseworthy—think about such things.

— PHILIPPIANS 4:8

7 MAY

Dear Friends,

Last month my husband and I were on a trip that was to include several cities. At least we thought it was—we hadn't counted on strep throat. After my slightly sore throat worsened and morphed and expanded north and south into my head and chest, I spent a week in a beautiful hotel room with what became the most expensive sore throat in family history.

Now listen, you who say, "Today or tomorrow we will go to this or that city . . . Instead you ought to say, "If it is the Lord's will, we will live and do this or that." (James 4:13,15) The whole experience was a maddening but needed reminder that we do not have the freedom to go where we want when we want. We are His, and God dictates where we go and when.

It has lately occurred to me that we don't have the freedom to go where we want to go in our thinking either. There are certain places to which God leads us, and there are others we are directed to avoid—Worry. Meanness. Pettiness. Envy. Fear. Rehashing mistakes or slights.

I have always thought that since I can't control what thoughts come I won't have to answer for them. But we are accountable for our thought lives. We may not have control over what thoughts come, but we do have control over where we linger in our thinking. We need to master our minds. We can train ourselves to immediately and resolutely reject any thoughts that are clearly not from Him.

And we can ask Him to do what we cannot do ourselves. A recent entry in my prayer journal says this: "You're teaching me what it means to take captive every thought to make it obedient to Christ. (2 Corinthians 10:5) A captive cannot go wherever it wants. It is constrained. Restrained. Restricted to a certain area. Certain parameters."

This is apparently a long-standing lesson for me. Yesterday I came across another entry, this one from years ago:

"April 4, 2004 When I commit to love the Lord my God with all my heart, soul and mind, it means all my mind, without reserving a section of it for things that are opposed to Him. All my mind is to be His. I do not have the right or the freedom or the privilege of letting my thoughts go where they want. God is the Owner/Proprietor/Master of my thought life."

This is coming up so often lately that I know this is where I need to focus my efforts and prayers right now. Spiritual battles are fought and won or lost in our thought lives. When we get our thinking under control—His control—we will be powerful, safe and strong.

Thinking of you,
Laura

Lord, I am Yours. Keep drawing my thoughts back to You and Your truth. Guard my mind against any thought or idea that would lead me away from the peace that is in You alone. May I be quick to discern and reject false thinking. I ask this for my safety and Your glory. Amen.

Listen to me,
. . . you whom I have upheld since you were conceived,
and have carried since your birth.
Even to your old age and gray hairs I am he,
I am he who will sustain you.
I have made you and I will carry you;
I will sustain you and I will rescue you.

—ISAIAH 46:3–4

14 MAY

Dear Friends,

In a movie I like, a woman sits on a couch curled up against her boyfriend (who happens to be President of the United States). And what's she doing? She's reading a biography of him! In fact, she's into Volume 2. She's apparently been at this a long time. And I want to say, "Close the book, honey! He's right beside you! Talk to him. Ask him questions. You can get to know him directly."

Summer is just ahead and the impulse may be to grab a book or devotional for summer study to keep ourselves spiritually alert. And it's a good idea. But book in hand or not, when you find yourself on the beach towel or standing at the grill or in the car or plane on the way to your vacation spot this summer, don't forget prayer. Simple conversation. Ask Him your questions, tell Him your fears. Tell Him a joke. Talk to the Man!

These days it often feels that there are just too many middle men between God and me. Authors. Clergy. Christian "experts." Sometimes I have to turn off the radio and put down the book and close my eyes and just be quiet. That can be hard to do, but I want His direct touch. I want the word He has that's just for me. I want Christ Himself, full strength and undiluted. He's right here and loving me, but too often I'm missing it. I'm too busy reading the latest best seller about Him or talking about Him or writing about Him or studying Him in a workbook.

When the Israelites were headed off to the Promised Land, God said that He would not go with them but He would send His angel along and they would be perfectly safe. But Moses wouldn't settle for an angel. He wanted God with them and nothing less. He insisted upon it. *If Your Presence does not go with us, do not send us up from here.* (Exodus 33:15) And the Lord agreed.

He is with you as you head into summer. He is with you because He wants to be. He created you for this very reason—He wanted a relationship with You. May none of us settle for anything less than direct engagement with Him who loves us so much and so eagerly anticipates our prayer conversation.

Force yourself to create those periods of quiet and attentiveness we need in order to hear His voice. All summer long allow Him to remind you of His presence with you and His command of your situation, whatever it may be. Keep bringing your mind back to these wonderful truths, and rest in them.

Have a magnificent summer!

Laura

For all we are learning of You, Lord, and for Your presence with us, we thank You. Amen.

...

Year Three

...

Renew a steadfast spirit within me.

— PSALM 51:10

3 SEPTEMBER

Dear Friends,

Today we witnessed the renewal of our friends' wedding vows. They have been married for twenty-five years. All five of their children participated in the beautiful Orthodox Jewish ceremony and four of the five, including their severely disabled son, held up the chuppah under which they stood. No doubt they cried joyful tears at their wedding in 1982, but today's tears were very different ones. They know the victory that this recommitment represents. They know from sharp experience what marriage asks of them and will ask. And they are saying yes. And it is a good thing and it is a hard thing and it is the right thing.

In 1988 I accepted Christ's forgiveness. This was no intellectual "decision for Christ" or "commitment to live for Him." Someone took the time to explain to me what Jesus had been doing on the cross, and I grasped for the first time that His sacrifice had been made for me. It spared me a deserved punishment. I saw Jesus that day for who He really is. And in that light I saw myself that day for who I really was. Both truths shocked me. A sinner faced her Savior. But the bitter truth of who I am was blanketed by the astounding truth of who He is. My complete forgiveness had been secured and was being held out to me, and I lunged to accept it with awe and relief. I accepted what had been done for me and I acknowledged that it needed to be done. Christ became my Savior.

It took some years, though, for me to grasp what His Lordship means and requires of me. In 1994, during an angry time after an unexpected loss, it took me days to recognize that I was wrestling not with the loss itself but with Him-who-controls-all-things. Another moment of decision. Was I willing to accept His sovereignty?

It was a hard time of prayer and surrender. But it led me to a deep, more considered commitment to Him and His Lordship.

Lord and Savior. Savior and Lord. Years may separate our understanding of those two titles and realities. How many of us, when we accept His forgiveness, understand what we are agreeing to? It is far easier to promise to follow when we don't know what's ahead than when we do. The pledges made once we know the cost must be particularly sweet and precious to Him, the promises made with eyes wide open. Recommitments have experience and knowledge and loss behind them. They are solemn treasure.

How long has it been since you first pledged yourself to live with Him and for Him and by His enabling? Has it been what you expected? Can you remember life without Him? This week in prayer thank Him again. Relive favorite memories from your life together. Remember the hard parts. Renew your vows. He has pledged His love to you for all time.

with you in Him,
Laura

May I be faithful to You who are called Faithful and True. Fix my eyes upon You and lead me according to Your will. Thank You, Savior. Thank You, Lord. Amen.

But I tell you who hear me . . .

— LUKE 6:27

10 SEPTEMBER

Dear Friends,

I had ears to hear but didn't hear. Last May my ear doctor found that a piece of dead skin was covering my eardrum. After a few weeks of eardrops he was able to remove it without pain or difficulty, and I could hear again; a hearing test confirmed it.

Hearing requires more than having ears. Those ears have to be in good working order, though even that isn't always enough—any parent of a child or teen knows that a pair of healthy, unobstructed ears is no guarantee of hearing. The distinction is made repeatedly in the Bible between 'those with ears' and 'those with ears to hear.' Thousands of people heard Christ teaching when He walked the earth but not all of them heard His message. And not all who heard His message heeded it. The same remains true today. His greatest promises are apprehended by those who listen and hear and heed what He is saying.

Our hearing may be blocked, as mine was. All sorts of lifeless things set themselves up against the knowledge of God—godless chatter, complaining, arguing, harshness, conceit, *"an unhealthy interest in controversies and quarrels"* (1 Timothy 6). These voices will most readily be recognized as false by those most familiar with the True voice. They'll know His voice from experience, from time in His presence. Ears that hear are ears attuned to the sound of God's voice. They are practiced in hearing it because they have devoted time to the quietness that such familiarity requires.

Even those who know Him may occasionally mistake a false voice for the real thing. Years ago we had a pastor from Illinois who had relocated to California. One of his friends, knowing how much he missed home, gave him a tape called "Sounds of the Midwest" and he happily fell asleep to that recording of birdcalls and train whistles and crickets. The next morning he woke to cacophony, and he opened his front door to find hundreds of crickets jostling for space on the doorstep, each of them lured by that counterfeit call to home and true love.

When my hearing was tested, I had to listen most attentively. Many of the sounds I listened for were subtle ones. I wore noise-cancelling headphones and sat in a soundproof booth. The audiologist went to those lengths to ensure that distracting, competing noises had been eliminated, and we who would know God's voice need to do the same. Are we willing to abide silence? It is a discipline rarely cultivated and not much valued these days. But in the quiet of our daily prayer time, as we listen attentively and with expectancy, we will learn to distinguish His from all the other voices coming at us; we will know that voice of truth, so often small and still.

Hear and heed. Wait and wash. Ears sensitive to spiritual truth are ears washed frequently in living water, the Word of God.

Here as His,
Laura

We would hear You, Lord. May we quiet ourselves, attend and obey. For Your glory. Amen.

. . . the Father himself loves you because you have loved me . . .

—JOHN 16:27

17 SEPTEMBER

Dear Friends,

We traveled a great distance last week to visit my in-laws in Greece. It is a country not my own, and they speak a language in which I stutter and am hesitant. Even after almost twenty-five years of visits I don't have enough grasp of the language or culture to always know what's going on around me or how to interpret what I see. Nevertheless, I am at home here because I am welcomed and I am loved. My favorite fruits are in the fridge, invariably a new nightgown in a cellophane wrapper is on a bedroom chair for me when I arrive. At the beach, a gaggle of grandmas approaches to greet me. Some of them I recognize and others I don't, but they know me.

Many gestures in this culture are social rituals enacted out of habit and for the eyes of others. But today I open a drawer of my father-in-law's desk in search of a pencil and find a small, well-worn photo of my son as a young child—a token of devotion hidden away and not intended for the world to see. A touching glimpse into a private, sincere heart.

This is a place where my son is known and loved. The entire house is a continually updated exhibit of his life. Everywhere I look are photos of him, childhood toys, remnants of summer visits, evidence that he has been here. His handiwork is on the walls and bookshelves. He is talked about with affection and laughter. His exploits and visits and phone calls are recalled and revisited often in conversation. When I play a recording for my mother-in-law of his singing, she smiles at the sound of his voice and nods and begins to cry. He is known and loved and longed for. His eventual return to this house is happily anticipated.

My in-laws are precious to me for many reasons, but primary

among them is this: I love them because they love my son. They share my delight in him and my pride. They remember many of the episodes of his life as clearly as I do. They abide my bragging and then top it with bragging of their own. They see wonderful things in him.

I think about the lengths to which we go to prove our devotion or usefulness to God. How earnestly we work for Him and polish our Christian image and wave our spiritual resumé. We sometimes forget this central, calming truth: He loves us dearly and always will, not for what we do for Him but because we love His Son.

In small ways and large, in public displays and private moments of communion, we live out our love for His Son. The Son is known and precious to us. And because we share in His life, more and more over time our relationships and conversation and character will display Him. More and more old décor and habits and choices will make way for mementos of Him and our life with Him and in Him. He will see to that. Our part is to entrust ourselves and our lives and our loved ones to Him day by day in our prayer conversation. Our part is to share our fears and joys and victories and questions, to rest in who we are as His. Our part is to give Him our time (we call it our time, He calls it His). The time we think of as our own is too often spent in busy busy busywork trying to earn what is already ours.

> With you in Him,
> Laura

Lord Jesus, I look back and see great evidence of Your transforming love. I look ahead and have such hope. You are before me and behind. I am Yours. I am home. Amen.

Because you are my help, I sing in the shadow of your wings.

—PSALM 63:7

24 SEPTEMBER

Dear Friends,

It has been a week of reunions—reunions with loved friends and relatives of my husband, and reunions with persistent and hated tendencies in myself. Mean thoughts and bitter words that I thought long vanquished have only been in hiding just waiting for a tired or weak moment to return and poison the visit with my in-laws. I pray the same old prayers I have prayed so often for forgiveness, for patience, for new responses to old challenges. I feel the same old despair at this revelation and reminder of who I am apart from Christ.

After a challenging morning, my husband and I took a drive on Tuesday to Corinth, only an hour away. On the way I read aloud from Paul's first letter to the Corinthians. The remains of the ancient city are extensive, excavated over decades since 1896 by the American School of Classical Studies. Paul visited here three times, it is thought, and while in Corinth he wrote his letters to the Romans and to the church at Ephesus.

Corinth has been an important city throughout history due both to its geographic position and to the composition of its soil. Pottery has been manufactured here for thousands of years because the pale Corinthian clay is exceptionally malleable and excellent for pottery making.

In the museum, hundreds of objects are displayed, including bronzes and marble and jewelry, and even intact glassware, as well as the perfectly formed and glazed clay objects one would expect. But I was drawn to another case, one that displayed shelves of misshapen vases and pots. These vessels that were malformed on the wheel or wrecked in the firing process were likely thrown away at that time but were discovered and retrieved long after by archeologists. Rejected as useless initially, they have had just as much to teach students of archeology and history and glazing techniques as the pristine articles among which they are displayed. I find them beautiful and encouraging and am grateful for their survival and inclusion in the exhibit.

Driving home, we pass acre upon acre of charred tree stumps, evidence of the summer fires. Wide black stripes cut across green hills and I think again of how my responses and black moods so often mar what would otherwise be beautiful. I pray another apology and veer again toward despair. But there is more than ash and charcoal on the hillside. Incredibly, greenery already is visible here and there, poking through the soil. In fact, there are hints of green in every direction. But the sharpest, most beautiful greenery springs up against the blackness of a dead forest. These are the signs of growth and new life that draw my eye.

The most breathtaking reminders of God's mercy and unfailing love come in those moments when I know myself to be most unlovable and undeserving. As we drive along, my prayers shift from me to Him, from who I am to who He is. And my eyes are raised up and my head and my heart and my praise are raised up.

evergreen with you in Him,
Laura

You shine and shine and shine out of the darkness, lighting our way. Thank You for who You are. We pray in Jesus' name, we pray as Your loved ones. Amen.

. . . if I have a faith that can move mountains,
but have not love, I am nothing.

— 1 CORINTHIANS 13:2

1 OCTOBER

Dear Friends,

Midday on Friday in the British Museum café, my husband and I sat down with tea at a long table, grateful for the rest and a snack. The three men to my right were involved in an animated, almost aggressive discussion about religion, the church, Christianity. They seemed not to know one another. I felt annoyance start to rise in me at some of what I heard. Finally, when the man beside me demanded with some impatience, "But what did Jesus ever say that wasn't also said by Buddha?" I jumped in, uninvited. "He said, *'I am the way, and the truth, and the life. No one comes to the Father except through me.'* He died to secure God's forgiveness for us, to pay our debt. Buddha didn't die for you."

The others chimed back in then, and more questions and answers flew and I left them to it. But I turned back to my tea disturbed by my tone and attitude. The man had stated a sincere question clearly and earnestly. It had provided a perfect opening to share some of the truth of what I know, and I had done so. But I had spoken with impatience and annoyance. I had aimed to win the point. As I rose to leave moments later, the man kindly offered my husband and me a pair of tickets he couldn't use for a museum lecture that evening. He was more gracious than I had been.

For Christ's love compels us Paul said to the Corinthians. (2 Corinthians 5:14). Christ's love compels us. His love is to be our motive and offering and fuel. But it had not been mine that day, and I had known it right away. My aim had been to win. I had the answer, I knew the truth, and I was going to make sure this dummy knew it, too!

Earlier in the week I had had a similar realization. In the midst of praying for some worn-out parents and troubled kids for whom I pray, I stopped. I was hearing myself once more ask God to help them. And I had stopped to consider, "What are you asking Him to do exactly? And what about you? In their need, where do you fit in, Laura?" I wrote this in my prayer journal that day:

"As I think today about these struggling parents and children, I pray in a new way. Instead of 'please provide for them,' today I add 'and may I do my part, too.' May I love them. In action. Not stand apart and shake my head, secretly thankful that this isn't my child. May I be willing to be part of the answer to my own prayers for them. Whom am I expecting to do it? May I love them in. May my kindness and love make You irresistible. You say in Jeremiah that you have drawn me with loving kindness. May the loving kindness you use to draw others be my loving kindness. May they know You because they know me. All my prayers for them have been, 'You, You, You, Lord. Do something. Save them.' And please do. But may I do my part. May those in trouble hear Your love in my voice and feel it from me. Then they'll run to You with eagerness. May they be loved into Your arms. By me."

Throughout the museum last week I saw numerous hand mirrors on display, some dating from hundreds of years before Christ. I noticed them because each one I saw reminded me that God never holds up a mirror to show us something unlovely in ourselves without holding in His other hand the solution for it. His intention is never condemnation but renovation.

learning to love,
Laura

Lord Jesus, thank You for Your love and for every opportunity You give us to share it, to demonstrate it, by what we say and what we do. Amen.

You hear, O LORD, the desire of the afflicted;
you encourage them and you listen to their cry . . .

—PSALM 10:17

8 OCTOBER

Dear Friends,

I can't for the life of me remember what I took to the hospital twenty-one years ago to serve as my "focal point" during childbirth. Probably because I never glanced at it. I suspect I threw it under the bed early in the proceedings. I was laboring with a ten-pound baby. I didn't need an inanimate focal point. What I needed was a serious dose of narcotics.

What I got instead was encouragement and continual reminders from my husband and the staff about what was ahead—that baby, yet unseen. "It won't be long!" "You're going to be holding him or her in your arms very soon." It didn't stop the pain but it refocused my thoughts on where they needed to be.

Several loved ones are facing extreme challenges. Each one is poised to step into an unfamiliar, unwelcome chapter of life. The circumstances vary but anxious thoughts are common to all. It has long puzzled me that "fear not" is the most oft-repeated command in the Bible. How can God ask us not to fear since He knows we can't control what feelings come? Even Jesus Himself was likely fearful in the Garden as He considered what was ahead. I wonder if with each "fear not" God is addressing our focus more than our feelings.

Several verses urge us to fix our eyes or our thoughts on Christ— off of what is seen and onto what is unseen. *Let us fix our eyes on Jesus* (Hebrews 12:2) is literally translated from the Greek "let us look away to Jesus." It suggests both turning from the present challenge and turning to Christ.

Prayer is our great gift in this, our immediate means of focusing on Christ—not some inanimate object but the Living God, the One with all power. We lift our eyes from our earthly circumstances and refocus on Him who has complete sovereignty over those circumstances. Our greatest weapon against fear is a focus on God. When we review His attributes, we remember what is eternally true about Him. When we read the psalms, there He is, line by line, in all His magnificence. When we recall His past works recorded throughout the Bible and recorded in the memories of our personal pasts, we remind ourselves of who He is and whose we are and what is eternally significant and what is not.

Take courage! It is I. Don't be afraid Jesus told His disciples as He walked across the water to them. (Matthew 14:27). More accurately it is translated, "Take courage. I AM. Don't be afraid." The very title by which Almighty God identified Himself to Moses at the burning bush is the one by which He identified Himself to the disciples and by which He identifies Himself to you and me in our every prayer conversation. What is ahead for you in this week? You are neither facing it alone nor limited to your own strength. Look away to Him!

co-laboring with you,
Laura

You hear our every cry. You are present with us and are ruling in all things. Thank You. May we trust You. Eternal, unchanging, unfailingly loving God, we praise Your name. Amen.

For the Lord gives wisdom, and from his mouth
come knowledge and understanding.

—PROVERBS 2:6

15 OCTOBER

Dear Friends,

Several weeks ago my husband and I sat at breakfast in Greece with old friends. Suddenly we almost leapt to our feet at the violence of an explosion that shook every table on the patio and rattled everyone's glassware and nerves. The waiter hurried over.

"There is no cause for concern. It is only dynamite."

Only dynamite. There were rock quarries nearby. But more likely local fisherman were blast fishing. Dynamite fishing is an illegal, quick way for fishermen to fill their boat and meet the day's quota. The shockwaves from the dynamite or homemade bombs kill or stun schools of fish, which are then are easily scooped up. This method of fishing has been in use for decades all over Southeast Asia, coastal Africa and the Aegean.

I couldn't help but think of Christ's promise to Peter and Andrew as He walked past and saw them cast their net into the Sea of Galilee. *"Come, follow me," Jesus said, "and I will make you fishers of men." At once they left their nets and followed him.* (Mark 1:17-18)

But what if they hadn't followed Him? What if, instead of following, they decided to go out among their neighbors in their own strength and according to their own business plan? What if, in their eagerness to be the best, to bring in the greatest haul of converts, those fishers of men had resorted to dynamite fishing? It seems today that many do. We all have loved ones who have sworn off church after having been stunned or blasted by someone determined to "win" them, convert them, convince them. I had one or two such encounters myself in college and swore that whatever they had or believed I wanted none of it.

With the best of intentions we sometimes go about the right thing in the wrong way. How foolish and counterproductive to proceed apart from His timing or say-so. When we remember that the most-needed word is not ours but His, we will spend as much time (and even more) talking to Him about our needy loved ones as we do talking to them about Him. Spending time in prayer for those in need is the vital prerequisite to anything else we might do for them. As the only possible Author of true faith, He is the One with whom we must be in conversation for unbelieving loved ones. And if we want to be used by Him in others' lives, we must be at prayer—He can direct our steps only if we are allowing Him to lead us.

Our willingness to set aside time for prayer signals to God a willingness to do things His way, at His pace. It is our bow to our Sovereign.

with you lured and led and loved,

Laura

Thank You for our lifetime of Your hearing and steering and cheering us on. May we be careful to follow Your leading as we live in Your name and love in Your name. Thank You, Lord, for your patient instruction. In Jesus' name. Amen.

How great is your goodness, which you have stored up
for those who fear you . . .

—Psalm 31:19

22 October

Dear Friends,

Yesterday I had a gift to give. I had spent several weeks preparing something for my son's birthday, a small scrapbook of impressions and family stories, photos, favorite quotes and memorabilia. I looked forward to giving it to him and had waited to do so in person.

I carried the package with me all day waiting for my moment, but yesterday was not the day. Pete was worn out from a cold and bothered by a sports injury. His thoughts were elsewhere, his mind on next year's housing situation and an upcoming exam and a special date that evening. We had a nice walk together and parted, arranging to meet up again this morning.

Today was the day. After a good sleep and meal and conversation I presented the gift, and he looked through it appreciatively. Timing may not be everything, but in this case it made all the difference. Yesterday the gift was wrapped and ready and in my hand, but the recipient was not ready to receive it.

What of the gifts God gives? I wonder if He holds something in His hand for me awaiting my undivided attention. Is He watching for His moment? Does He wait with eagerness until I turn His way, my heart open and receptive? If His aim is our greatest blessing, and it is, He will certainly ensure that the moment when His gifts come to us will be ideal. Am I hampering or delaying any blessing? Am I missing out on things because my attitude or attention have wandered from Him? What are my eyes and thoughts fixed upon? What does He await?

I could have mailed my son's gift or left it in his room to be found later, but most of my joy in giving came in anticipating and witnessing his pleasure in it. I happily sat beside him as he leafed through the book, and enjoyed his discovery of small, funny details. We laughed together. I want to offer that same joy to the Giver of every good gift. When He gives me gifts—talents, health, family, sustenance, opportunities—I want to include Him in my enjoyment of them, and allow Him to share in the moment. And prayer, our ongoing conversation with one another, offers the opportunity for exactly that kind of sharing between us.

blessed with you in Him,
Laura

We need never enjoy Your gifts in solitude. Thank You for how eager You are to join in and play along and show us how they work. May we call You into our every blessing. Amen.

You came near when I called you, and you said, "Do not fear."

— LAMENTATIONS 3:57

29 OCTOBER

Dear Friends,

I am grateful to have been away from home last week as fires burned throughout southern California. At my safe remove, I probably prayed more than I would have had I been home and in the thick of it. Having been spared many of the necessary tasks and decisions and the immediate and fearsome reality of it, I'm sure I was more composed than I would have been otherwise. And I prayed.

Throughout the week in the many conversations with my husband and friends, particularly after the evacuation order was lifted, I was aware of their great need to talk it out. Stories were told and retold. In crises, good or bad, the need is to talk and talk about it, to share details, to hear it spoken. Putting it into words makes it real and relieves us of it in some way.

It seemed all week that every time I opened the Bible I came upon verses that mentioned God's compassion or comfort. Comfort is ours when someone is willing to draw near and to listen. What we most need to know when we are threatened or hurting is that we are not alone and that our pain is heard. And our God urges us over and over to turn Godward and to share with Him all that we need to speak. *Pour out your heart like water in the presence of the Lord.* (Lamentations 2:19) Comfort is ours through prayer.

And of course He is so much more than a willing ear. He is also the One with every needed solution. Unlike well-meaning friends, He can direct our steps unfailingly and He wants to. He is Almighty God. And so we can turn to Him not only for comfort, but also for leading in the very midst of the crisis. Guidance is ours in prayer.

We can rest in the knowledge that He controls the situation entirely. He is mighty over it. However chaotic or senseless it appears,

He is accomplishing His purposes with compassion and intentionality. We can trust Him in this. Even when we are not offered answers to "Why?" we are offered this certain knowledge: He is at once entirely sovereign and unfailingly loving. This assurance is ours as we spend time in conversation with Him.

Faced with the magnitude of those fires, the power, the breadth, with every report of flame and uncontrolled wind, what came to my mind repeatedly were the apostles' words of amazement and relief, *"Even the winds and the waves obey him!"* (Mark 4, Matthew 8, Luke 8). "He is controlling this," I kept reminding myself.

He was overpowered by nothing last week as over 500,000 acres burned. He was Master over all that took place. And He was accomplishing something in it. We have been allowed another sobering, thrilling glimpse both of our own true powerlessness and of His incredible might. And we have been given another opportunity to thank Him for our position of safety as His.

safe with you in Him,
Laura

We praise You, Almighty God, God of all might. We praise You, too, as the God of all comfort. Thank You for who You unchangingly are. All Your power is at work not against us but on our behalf, and we thank You. We come to You in prayer with thankful hearts and with relief. Amen

I am still confident of this: I will see the goodness
of the LORD in the land of the living.

—Psalm 27:13

5 November

Dear Friends,

I visited recently with my long-time friend Clara, a talented painter. I asked her about her perspective as an artist. I know she tends to look at her surroundings in terms of light and shadow and color and texture. On a walk together, as we passed trees and reservoir and birds, she likely saw them differently than I did. But, she told me, the artist's perspective is something that can be learned. She has been able to convey it to her husband over the years as they've spent time together and she has shared her perspective. Her way of seeing has, to a large extent, become his.

Early last week I visited my hometown, a village I haven't seen in years. With adult eyes I saw it entirely differently than I did as a child. I had a new appreciation for the beautiful dense woods and low stone walls that line the roads, both of which I likely took entirely for granted when I lived there. I also found myself evaluating the area in terms of property taxes, the quality of the schools, the accessibility of services, things never considered in childhood. My perspective is very changed. The child has returned as an adult, as a homeowner, as a parent.

We can consider things from a variety of stances. As maturing Christians, a spiritual perspective should prevail more and more as we regard the state of the world and the circumstances of our lives. The spiritual perspective is not merely one view selected from many possible views, it is the view of things that matters, the one that is most comprehensive and true. It is the view that includes God, the unchanging, all-powerful, benevolent Ruler over all that happens.

A spiritual take on things eases one's way. When we think in terms of eternity, today's concerns diminish in intensity. When we lift our eyes, the immediate loses its urgency. If we are going to stay ahead of despair or mental exhaustion, the long view is the one that's needed.

But the godly view of things is more than a source of emotional strength or comfort. It is a choice that lays the most secure, unshakable foundation from which one can step out into the world each day. The life that is attuned to Christ's presence and purposes and movement is a usable life, a life at the ready. It is hopeful and trusting; it is a life that can look beyond troubling circumstances and wait, with eyes fixed on Him.

Adopting such a perspective is not something we have to sweat and work at. It comes as naturally as the child view maturing into the adult's. It is a gentle shift of perspective that results from time spent with Jesus Christ. Lives of prayer are those that intentionally, intricately entwine themselves with His by continual conversation and checking in. As we discipline ourselves to live praying lives, to become increasingly conscious of His presence, to daily share with Him our thoughts, concerns, reactions and hopes, and allow Him to do the same, His perspective, more and more, becomes our own.

eternally His, with you,
Laura

Lord, You are called by Paul the blessed and only Ruler. You rule in all the circumstances of my life. Nothing is transpiring except by Your will. May I work with You, in trust, and not against You, in fear. May I not miss any of what You're doing around me by forgetting Your hand in it. Thank You for the opportunities daily to know You better as I witness Your power and provision. In Jesus' name and for Your honor, Amen.

Search me, O God, and know my heart; test me and know
my anxious thoughts. See if there is any offensive way in me,
and lead me in the way everlasting.

—PSALM 139:23-24

12 NOVEMBER

Dear Friends,

King David lived his life acutely, gratefully, conscious of God's presence with him and of the honor and praise and obedience that are His due. David is known for many things, and chiefly for his passion to know God and to honor Him. God Himself calls David *"a man after my own heart"* (Acts 13:22). David opened up his life to God sharing everything—his thoughts, his needs, his joys and requests. He wrote song after song praising God. More than seventy of the 150 psalms have been attributed to David. He also wrote songs seeking God's leading and protection and forgiveness. Over and over he demonstrated that he knew where to turn in times of challenge. When the people had turned against David, and even spoke of stoning him, 1 Samuel 30:6 tells us that *David strengthened himself in the LORD his God.* In one of his most beautiful psalms of praise and worship, Psalm 138, David offers a memorable and beautiful line of thanks to God saying, *my strength of soul you increased.*

David wanted to know God, and he sought to honor Him by dedicating all that he had and all that he was to God. He knew that to make such an offering required that he examine his life and heart because he wanted it to be a clean life, a usable life that He offered. But David also knew the insufficiency of self-examination. There is much in each of us that we cannot know; the human heart is deceitful. We are, for example, often unconsciously guided by self-serving motives. Jeremiah 17:9-10 tells us that *the heart is deceitful above all things and beyond cure. Who can understand it? I the Lord search the heart and examine the mind.* We can deceive ourselves and others but we cannot deceive God. Who we are is open before Him. And so it was God whom David asked to examine his heart. He asked God to do what only God can.

A great gift is available to us in prayer—the truth about ourselves. Someone ready to hear the truth about themselves will not necessarily hear it from a human counselor but they will hear it from God. They will hear it if they will allow themselves to be examined by Him and will quiet themselves to hear the findings. A willingness to report to prayer is a willingness to face oneself. We will hear from our Creator what we will never hear from our mother, our mentor, our guru, our pal. And along with the truth offered in love will be the solution offered in love. He alone can do something about what He alone can see in us, so we would be foolish not to listen. We, thankfully, can change. He, thankfully, will not.

Have you a secret wish to be completely known and completely loved? That secret wish is fulfilled in Christ and in Him alone, our Savior, our friend.

> Known to Him,
> Laura

Thank You, Father, for your refusal to leave us as we are, who we are, where we are. For Your promise never to lay down the work You have begun in us until it is completed, we thank You. For who You are, for all we have in You, we praise Your name, Almighty God. Amen.

I was a stranger and you invited me in . . .

— MATTHEW 25:35

19 NOVEMBER

Dear Friends,

As a new bride I wanted to do everything just right. Long before I would have had the nerve to try roasting a turkey, I decided I probably could manage roasting a chicken. The recipe told me to "wash the chicken and pat it dry." So I washed it thoroughly. With dish soap. Lemon Joy. My husband, accustomed to Greek-style chicken cooked with lemon, congratulated me. He thought it tasted great . . . even after I told him that I hadn't actually used any lemons.

His job as a professor brought us invitations to university events of various kinds. I was eager to respond appropriately and received an invaluable bit of counsel from an older faculty wife. She said that when you want to thank your host or hostess after a party or dinner or event, it is customary to express your thanks in the same manner by which the invitation came to you. So if you were invited by phone, you call the day after the event and thank them by phone. If the invitation came in the mail, you write a note of thanks.

God has extended an invitation. Every one of us has chosen to go our own way in life, but He is so eager to be in relationship with us that He has provided a way for us to be restored to Him. He sent Christ to pay our sin debt on the cross and invites each one of us to accept that gift and to enter into a forgiven, relieved life as His. The invitation has been extended to each one of us, and individually we will accept it or we will not.

When we understand what He is offering, what He has done for us, and that our part is simple repentance and a "Yes!" we respond readily. And with amazed and grateful hearts. Thanks is due! And as time passes and we learn more of Him and all that He offers us as His, the more thankful we are, and the more we want to express our thanks.

Well, our old rule applies. We are to extend our thanks to Him in the same manner by which He extended His invitation to us.

He invited us to become His by giving His life for us. We thank Him by giving our lives to Him. We allow Him to use us, to steer us, to accomplish His loving purposes in this world through us.

He invited us lovingly. *I have drawn you with lovingkindness.* (Jeremiah 31:3) *I led them with cords of human kindness.* (Hosea 11:4) He invited me using the love of a friend who patiently walked alongside me for a long time. I thank Him by doing the same for another.

He invited us in by speaking to us, sometimes whispering, by sharing His heart. We thank Him by speaking to Him, by prayer.

He drew us to Him by sharing with us more and more of who He is. We thank Him by sharing with Him more and more of ourselves, our dreams, our gifts, our hopes, our lives.

We are the sometimes stumbling bride of Christ. But He is cheering us on, and continually offering all that we need to get it right.

What joy is ours!
Laura

Lord God, may our thoughts, our words, our lives as Yours reflect thankful hearts. Amen.

. . . my yoke is easy and my burden is light.

— MATTHEW 11:30

26 NOVEMBER

Dear Friends,

My Thanksgiving To Do list still sits on the counter, part of my plan for last week:

Pick up rolls at bakery; buy oranges; make cranberry sauce . .

In the car this morning, my husband mentioned how much he liked a verse we'd heard in church, 1 Thessalonians 5:16-18—an additional To Do list, this one God's plan for us:

Be joyful always; pray continually; give thanks in all circumstances, for this is God's will for you in Christ Jesus.

Give thanks in all circumstances? Buying rolls and fruit sound a lot easier. We spent Thanksgiving with our friends Jan and Warren, and Jan reminded me of circumstances a few years ago in which she wasn't feeling very thankful. Warren was out of town and she was home alone and doing yard work in dusty gardening clothes. Their house is isolated and set back quite a distance from the road, so when she hears an unfamiliar car approaching, as she did now, she is a bit wary. Solicitors and realtors are the ones who most often make the long trip in from the road and she did not welcome the approach or chatter of either.

The car came into sight and parked—an unfamiliar one as she'd expected. The driver hopped out and came around the front of the car, but instead of approaching Jan he opened the back door of the car and said the last thing she expected to hear, "Mr. Billy Graham would like to say hello," and out of the car stepped Billy Graham.

Jan greeted him and introduced herself. He was looking for Warren's parents, who had lived in this house years earlier but now live across the road. She delightedly led the way.

Jan's plan for the day was for housework and raking leaves.

God's plan included an afternoon of laughter and memorable conversation as her in-laws reminisced with an old friend. What arrived looking like an annoyance, intrusion, interruption, was a blessing intended by God. His blessings don't always come to us in familiar or welcome packages. His plan for our day very often is not our plan. But we can trust Him even when His hand in our circumstances is difficult to discern.

And notice how gently His plan for Jan's day unfolded. So it is with His plan that we be joyful always, pray continually and give thanks in all circumstances. These are not torturous challenges set for us or tasks we must strain to achieve. Joy and thankfulness and constant conversation with our Companion and Friend result naturally when we are mindful of God's presence with us, and His power over all our circumstances, and His unfailing love for us.

The more time we spend with Him the better we will know Him. The better we know him the more we will trust Him. The more we trust Him the more joyfully and thankfully and promptly we will yield to Him and His plan. And all these good things begin with time in His presence. They begin in prayer.

> with thanks to Him and
> love to you,
> Laura

Lord, may all Your purposes be accomplished in my life. May Your will be done entirely. Amen.

But our citizenship is in heaven.

—PHILIPPIANS 3:20

3 DECEMBER

Dear Friends,

Twenty-five years ago tomorrow my husband and I met at a Christmas party. He has lived in this country longer now than he ever lived in his native Greece. But however many years it will be, and despite his American citizenship of nearly twenty years, Greece will always be home. Part of the reason we moved to California were the familiar sights and scents in every direction—the hills and citrus trees, the light, the bougainvillea and hibiscus, the sun setting over the sea.

I remember that on the way to his naturalization ceremony our son quizzed his dad on the Pledge of Allegiance and our national anthem. "Wait, wait, tell me again, who's José?" my husband joked. "José, can you see…" We laughed, in a festive mood. As the time of the ceremony neared, though, he became serious and even sad. Many of the people becoming citizens cried through the ceremony. But the judge administering the oath offered well-chosen words of comfort. "We are not asking you to lay down your heritage, your customs, your love for your native land. Bring them with you,' he urged. "Enrich the rest of us by them. Broaden our world and understanding."

Exactly our commission as well. This world is not our home. We are ambassadors representing another land and here on assignment. We stand in for Christ Himself, acting as His earthly agents— the arms by which He comforts and lifts and carries, the hands by which He welcomes and feeds and holds others steady. Our heritage as His is the one that matters, the one we must retain, the one we are called to share when asked. *Always be prepared to give an answer to everyone who asks you to give the reason for the hope that you have.* (1 Peter 3:15)

Prayer is the phone card in our pocket. Prayer is our instant access to home when we're homesick, when the strain and pain of living in this alien culture threaten to overwhelm us. It is our clear connection to that Voice of truth, the one we most need to hear. We sit with Him in our prayer spot, our own private phone booth with room enough for two. We close all the books and quiet ourselves and close our eyes to this world and look to Him and tell all. And of course it is a two-way conversation. He responds to the outpouring of our hearts with an outpouring of His own heart.

As ambassadors, Prayer is our diplomatic pouch—the means by which He relays all that He has for us and all He would have us share with those among whom we live: Love, Joy, Peace, Patience, Goodness, Faithfulness, Patience and Self-Control—the customs and language and fruits of our native land.

resident alien with you,
Laura

Father, may Your kingdom come, may Your will be done on this earth as it is done in heaven. More and more may here be like there, and may I faithfully do my part in making it so. For the sake of Your honor and glory. Amen

The word is very near you; it is in your mouth
and in your heart so you may obey it.

— DEUTERONOMY 30:14

10 DECEMBER

Dear Friends,

When I was eleven, I had the great blessing of going to Texas to live with Big Laura. She and my grandfather had married early in my childhood though they were no longer together by this time. But blood tie or no, Laura and I had similar personalities and preferences and senses of humor, and we fell into a life together easily and happily. We even shared the same first name, so from the start we were Big Laura and Little Laura.

My first Christmas with Big Laura was memorable because that was the start of her Scripture Tree. Late in November, Big Laura had an idea for a new kind of Christmas tree. Instead of the usual evergreen, she cut and carried home a large, bare, silvery Texas persimmon branch that she covered with tiny white lights and secured in a deep pot of sand. She bought a stack of colored poster board, pens, glue and scissors and invited my friends and hers to come over and make ornaments. She showed us how to use a concordance, something I had never seen. We looked up words—hand or angel or candle or dove or heart—whatever we thought we could draw, and then chose a verse. Drawing and cutting out the shape, we wrote the verse on the front and our name on the back and hung each ornament on the tree with colored yarn.

The Scripture Tree was beautiful. As word got around, all sorts of people came by to see it. Big Laura was even interviewed on a local radio program. The following year she brought home an even larger branch and we added more ornaments. Eventually she left the tree up all year and by the time she died in 1993 it had stood in her living room for more than twenty years.

This evening, as I look again through the stack of Scripture Tree ornaments I made so many years ago, I marvel that before I had ever read the Bible, before I knew much about God or Christ, before I had begun to speak to Him very often, He already had begun to speak to me. I see what reassurances He extended to me as a child and what verses I was drawn to, what comfort I reached for, what truths I grabbed onto. *Fear not, for I am with you.* (Isaiah 41:10). *Be still and know that I am God.* (Psalm 46:10). *Ye are the light of the world.* (Matthew 5:14). *My times are in Thy hand.* (Psalm 31:15) *He shall give His angels charge over thee.* (Psalm 19:11) *The sun of righteousness shall rise.* (Malachi 4:2) And at the bottom of the stack I find a tiny rectangular scrap on which is written, simply, *I AM.*

Before we turn to Him, He is turned to us. Before we claim Him, He has claimed us. Even in the past before we knew Him, God was present in His full power and was making Himself known and was accomplishing His loving will. I am with you always, He says. Never past tense. Eternally present.

His even then, His even now,
Laura

Lord Jesus, Your name is the Word of God, and the word of God is living and active. Thank You that You are present with us and with our loved ones, even those who don't yet claim you. Amen

Jesus replied, "If anyone loves me, he will obey my teaching.
My Father will love him, and we will come to him
and make our home with him."

—JOHN 14:23

17 DECEMBER

Dear Friends,

I spent time this month preparing for my in-laws' arrival from Greece for the winter. I washed their favorite sheets and made chicken soup her way. I had the satellite dish reconnected that brings in TV channels in their own language. I bought bags of lentils and bunches of dandelion greens. I positioned the welcome mat that says, "Καλως Ηρθατε" ('we're glad you're here'). I searched for the bread and yogurt and toothpaste that would be closest to what they have and like at home. I worked at making it as familiar and home-like as I could.

Christ has promised to make His home in my heart, and I work to make it as comfortable as possible for Him to live in me. I want my heart to be His home away from home, a place where He can relax because He knows He will be protected there from offense or dishonor. I want it to be a place He shares His confidences because He trusts me with them and knows that I daily quiet myself to listen. In me I want Him to find Himself surrounded by what He most loves—a fridge full of fruits of the Spirit (peace, patience, kindness, ...) a heart as soft as a sofa with some give to it as He rests Himself there. An open place without dark corners. I have said before that I want my heart to be to Him what Mary and Martha's house was—His haven in a hard world, a place He can express Himself freely.

This week I realized that what makes this home for my in-laws are not only those things that I supply. Even more important will be the things that they bring with them. My mother-in-law opening her suitcase is like Mary Poppins opening her carpetbag—out come the village cheeses, her favorite robe, the soap she makes herself, seeds and cuttings from her home garden that she intends to plant and nurture here.

Jesus and His Father will come to you and me and make their home with us—what promise in that promise! *We will come to him and make our home with him.* What you or I strive to supply or to set right in ourselves are important, but are the lesser contributions. The important furnishings are all that they bring with them, all that they carry from home and bring into our hearts. Things foreign to us and thrilling and new, things we could never supply ourselves.

The renewal and renovation the Trinity have undertaken make our own hearts unrecognizable to us at times. We find new light, we come upon sweet things that weren't there before. They know best what they love best and they bring those things with them. They come into you and me with bags bursting with gifts and treasures from their heavenly home, and they set to work. They are making themselves a home, creating for themselves a place in which to live, to love, to laugh, to rest, a place from which to work in this world. And you and I, the glad beneficiaries, become places of great promise. Let every heart prepare Him room!

with you blessed and beautified,
Laura

Lord Jesus, we sing "Joy to the world, the Lord is come" because You are, You have, You're here. Our hearts say Hallelujah! Our hearts say Welcome Home.

He is wooing you from the jaws of distress to a spacious place free from restriction, to the comfort of your table laden with choice food.

— JOB 36:16

7 JANUARY

Dear Friends,

Last night was a night at our house I will long remember. Our dining table was surrounded by good friends and family and on it were nine or ten different dishes of rich, home-made, delicious food from which to choose. For five hours we sat at the table eating and laughing and talking and listening. Our four kids, all in their twenties, joined in the meal and the conversation and we heard about their lives at college and their thoughts about high school and the years that lie ahead. Long after we finished eating, we lingered at the table talking.

I'm sure our friends enjoyed their dinner, but the evening was particularly remarkable for my family and me. Here we were in the comfort of our own home, at our own table, able to promise our friends a wonderful meal, yet little more had been required of us than to set the table. My mother-in-law had spent days cooking the food, and with all of us in mind. My favorite of her dishes is the stuffed eggplant, and there it was. My husband's favorite casserole was made for him. Because my friend Barbara likes her spinach pie, my mother-in-law had hunted in several stores for the freshest, best-looking spinach. Peter got his chicken, and our vegetarian guests had special dishes prepared especially for them. We were served, we were fed, we were blessed. We only had to come to the table.

How beautifully this pictures what is ours in prayer. Our dining table happens to be the usual place for my morning prayer time and how fitting, for prayer is the laden home table at which we are fed. He who knows best what we most hunger for is the One able and most willing to provide it. He only awaits our joining Him there. We are His guests at prayer, we come at His invitation. Prayer is a lingering in one another's presence. Confidences are exchanged, new tastes are sampled and added to our favorites list. When we limit prayer to what we're doing there—praising, thanking, confessing, making requests—we miss so much. If we would consider what prayer is to Him we would run to His table with eagerness. He has so much to bring, to say, to convey, to bestow.

Close to midnight I stood in our driveway waving as our guests drove away. There was a lot to do before bed, dishes awaited me in the kitchen, but I stood waving. For years I've watched my in-laws do this—it is a small sacrifice but great gift to stand with hand raised as long as those departing are still in sight. It is a sign of love. It says you matter to me. Our time together is precious. I am not in a hurry to be away from you, to be done with this, to turn to my next task. Being with you is pleasure for me. I happily anticipate your return.

Standing there, I imagined that this is the Lord's posture as our prayer time ends—His eye on us, as ever, His hand raised in blessing as we go about the tasks of the day, in no hurry to be done with us, unwilling to turn from us, already planning His next menu.

richly fed with you in Him,
Laura

You, ever watching and ever waving Your loved ones along their way, may we honor You. Amen.

The Lord your God is with you, he is mighty to save.

—ZEPHANIAH 3:17

14 JANUARY

Dear Friends,

After visiting my friend Lupe not long ago, she offered to give me a ride back to my car, which was parked quite a distance away. As we were headed out of her house, her sister Martha said she'd like to ride along with us. Lupe and I caught each other's eye, amazed, and the three of us got into the car.

Most of that ten-minute drive was silent because Lupe and I were praying like mad— thanking God, marveling at what He can do, and praying for Martha.

Five months earlier, Martha, her husband and infant daughter had been in the worst bus accident in the history of Ensenada. The city bus in which they were passengers flipped, hit another vehicle, and was torn in two. Eight of the passengers on the bus were killed instantly and others died later. No one in either vehicle escaped severe injury or death. Martha was the most gravely injured in her family and by the time of my visit she had had multiple surgeries and grafts. But as severe as her physical injuries were, more incapacitating had become her understandable terror of riding in a car. Many people had been praying for a long time for her recovery— physical, psychological, emotional, spiritual. Her sudden willingness to join us for that short ride was nothing short of miraculous. It represented a tremendous milestone, and that brief car trip was a true joy ride.

No one driving past three women in a blue Toyota that day likely recognized God at work. But seen or unseen, He is at work all around us, all the time. I wonder how many of the seemingly mundane events we witness each day represent God's great victories.

When friend Devon kept coming to my mind in December, I prayed for her and her family. I sent an email to ask if everything was alright and her answer gave me pause: "Thank you for your extra prayers. Everything is okay here but I can't imagine what would be going on if you hadn't been praying."

I had never thought of it that way. God alone knows all that our prayers are accomplishing. He who calls us to pray in the first place knows where and why our prayers are needed and all that they are achieving or averting.

As you pray this week, acknowledge His visible and invisible work around and within us. Give Him the credit and thanks He deserves for all the losses, germs, accidents, and near-misses we unknowingly have been spared, and for all the ways He is protecting and healing and freeing and transforming us.

> He is living and active. Everywhere.
> Always. Hallelujah!
> Laura

Our Father who loves us, we praise You as God Almighty, mighty over all. We pray in Jesus' name. Amen.

Love one another. As I have loved you, so you must love one another.

— JOHN 13:34

21 JANUARY

Dear Friends,

We have had an intensely challenging week after my mother-in-law broke several bones last Monday falling off a ladder. But this family crisis is affording us an ongoing opportunity to put into practice all we are learning of prayer and patience.

How evident is God's love at times like these. Never are we more relieved by and grateful for the grasp of His hand as when we are groping around in fear and helplessness. As I told a friend this week, I don't enjoy these crises, but I do love all that they afford us spiritually. Reminders of our frailty—my in-laws' and ours—have been ubiquitous all week. (I couldn't for the life of me remember our house number to give the ambulance, a house we have lived in for sixteen years). Our focus and nerves all are scrambled. But these evidences of our vulnerability have been made bearable by the many assurances of His proximity and power. Our desperate "I can't!" is met by His "I can." And His even greater "I will." And "I already have."

At one point this week I was taken aback by what I was feeling. It was so unexpected. It was… joy! "How, in these horrendous circumstances, can I be feeling joy?" I wondered. But it was exactly because of the circumstances that I did. When we are so keenly aware of our own helplessness and our need for Him, and are reminded then of His presence and sufficiency, we can only praise Him for who He is and thank Him for all that is ours as His.

Early in the week, the family had to make a decision regarding surgery and there was no consensus. I prayed for accord among us and for God's clear leading, and I asked friends to pray the same. (A favorite prayer of mine is prayed by Jehoshaphat in 2 Chronicles 20

We do not know what to do, but our eyes are upon you.) Overnight we had a clear and obvious answer and the surgery was scheduled for Wednesday night and went beautifully.

Looking back, we see so many ways He was preparing us for last week and for the weeks of rehabilitation ahead. Seemingly minor decisions made months ago about the house and our schedules all were being orchestrated by Him and were putting in place necessary details for what is ahead. He not only is with us, He is way ahead of us.

I have never been more grateful for compassion in others and a kind word than I have been this week when we are so frazzled and tired. It has been a most important reminder that the greatest gifts we can offer one another, what are most needful, are mercy and loving kindness. The grace of God. Thank you for your prayers.

with you in Him,
Laura

Heavenly Father, lead us and feed us and carry us through. Thank You for every reminder of Your presence and love. May we work with You and not against You in any way, and may all Your will be done. Unchanging and True, we praise Your Name. Amen.

Hallelujah! For our Lord God Almighty reigns.
Let us rejoice and be glad and give him glory!

—REVELATION 19:6-7

28 JANUARY

Dear Friends,

What does it mean to say that God is sovereign? It means that He is the supreme, permanent authority in all things. All power is His. He controls all things. Good and bad things. He rules completely in all circumstances. No one and nothing can thwart or resist His plan. He is never overruled or defeated, no matter how things look in human terms.

We say we do, but do we truly believe this? Do we rather suspect that God sometimes is limited in how much He can do in a particular situation? Do we worry that His plans can be foiled by a defiant teen? An unbelieving spouse? Negative thinking? Politicians? Satan? Bad luck? Acts of nature? Unforeseen events?

Almighty God is limited by nothing and no one. He controls all things. All power is His. This issue of His sovereignty is vital; it must be our starting point as men and women of prayer. Until each of us has wrestled with and settled the question of God's sovereignty, praying with confidence and power is impossible. As Warren Wiersbe says, "How can I pray to a God who permits my life to be the victim of 'fate' or the plaything of 'chance' or 'luck'? Which of His many promises can I claim if He is unable to fulfill them?"

More important is this: we were created to worship God, to honor Him. He is worthy of all honor and glory. How can we give Him the praise He is due if we believe His power or influence are limited?

God is sovereign. He also is unfailingly loving. This certain knowledge will launch our prayers and our lives as His. And this truth will also be the haven we return to again and again all our lives when things seem to be spinning out of control and we are tempted to fear or despair.

How do we come to this certainty? We spend time with Him. We allow Him to tell us who He is. We read what He tells us about Himself in 1 Samuel 2:6-8, in 1 Chronicles 29:10-13, in 2 Chronicles 20:6, in Job 42:2, in Psalm 33:10-11, in Psalm 47:2, 7-8. We take Him at His Word, as Abraham did. *Abraham believed God and it was credited to him as righteousness.* (James 2:23) Believing God is a choice. It is a decision. It is a step of faith and a step of obedience.

If this issue of God's sovereignty is something you have not settled in your heart and mind, dedicate some prayer time to it. It is most important that you do. Sit with Him a while. Tell Him your doubts and questions. Ask Him all that you need to. Perhaps there are events in your life that you cannot reconcile with a loving God. Talk to Him about those. Give yourself time with Him. Give Him time to answer. Take time with Him tomorrow and talk some more.

The truth of Who He is is the great good news. Much more important than who we are. More lasting and true than our current circumstances. And the source of all our hope.

> The LORD—He is God!
>
> Laura

Almighty God, may we worship You in knowledge and truth, with grateful hearts. Amen.

Then he looked at those seated in a circle around him and said,
"Here are my mother and brothers!"

—MARK 3:34

4 FEBRUARY

Dear Friends,

I was taken aback this week by the comment of a friend, an east coast seminary student: "Seminary is not a place for spiritual growth." She is surrounded by men and women too preoccupied with ministry to spend time with God.

"We cannot serve the Lord. There is nothing we can offer Him," says Oswald Chambers. "But we can put ourselves in such a place that His power can flow through us." And that place must be a place of listening and of allowing Him to lead. It is a place of being still. It values what He does more than what we do.

Christ has something for us in private, extended prayer time that will not be ours any other place or way. *Among those who approach I will show myself holy.* (Leviticus 10:3) Of the ten lepers healed by Jesus, only one of them sought Him out to thank him. And he was the only one of the ten blessed with time alone with Christ and a personal word from Him. The personal word you most need is what He has for you in private prayer.

We can be very busy for God and out of touch with God. We can be so determined to serve Him our way that we are reluctant to slow down long enough to find out whether our plan is His. So we proceed without Him. "Great men do great things without prayer, but they are not great things of God."

A willingness to quiet ourselves and hear Him out says, "I am willing to relinquish my plan for Yours. What You want is important to me. What You have to say to me now matters more than anything else I would do with this time." *Speak, Lord, for your servant is listening.* (1 Samuel 3:10)

The One-on-one relationship that is the strength of our days (and the fuel of true corporate worship) is grown in private. A full focus on Christ is not possible in a crowd, even a crowd of worshippers. Praying or worshipping only in church or in groups would be like having only group dates or double dates with the love of your life, never being alone with him or her. How intimate and deep is the conversation or relationship going to get?

Leave some plan of yours undone today to check in with Him. He is in place and patiently awaiting you with just the word you need of counsel and steering and relief.

Love,
Laura

Holy One, may I value You and Your will over me and my own. With You is where I most need to be. Get me there. Overrule anything that would keep me from time with You. In Jesus' name. Amen.

I will remember the deeds of the LORD; yes,
I will remember your miracles of long ago.

—PSALM 77:11

11 FEBRUARY

Dear Friends,

During your daily prayer time, try writing out your prayers. Not just requests, but everything—praises, thanks, confession, every thought, question, concern shared with Him. Trying this has been a tremendous boost to my prayer time with God. Writing as you pray may feel false at first but I urge you to keep at it over several days. The writing will become second nature. You need not be eloquent, grammatical, neat, or even coherent. Putting pen to paper simply keeps you focused on the conversation at hand. It forces the mind to attend. I use small, inexpensive spiral notebooks for my prayer time and when a stray thought comes—get milk. call Helen—I simply record it at the top of the page and then get right back to prayer.

Prayer draws us nearer to Him. It reminds us of our relationship and of His power and proximity. It puts our cares in perspective. I kept journals for 35 years but writing out my prayers produces a different sort of journal. It is the record of a conversation, the ongoing chronicle of a deepening relationship. The Old Testament records many instances of people setting up altars or stone markers at the place where they saw God perform a mighty act. Your prayer notebook will become just such a tangible memorial to God's work in your life. You will have a record of prayers and answers, of shared confidences—a memory book of the central love story of your life. I know of a woman who ends her prayer time each and every morning by writing a thank-you note to God. King David wrote out His prayers, and how we blessed we are that he did. We call his love letters to God the book of Psalms.

Your prayer journal will also be a precious record of your life with and love for family members, friends, anyone for whom you are praying. It is Sunday evening now, only hours after the passing of Betty Jo Lewis, beloved friend and prayer mentor to so many of us. How grateful I am for the record I have of my prayers for her as well as some of her own thoughts:

She said in 2004, "God really wants to take each of us to be with Him, so if He leaves me here it's because He has a mission for me here. We have work to do for Him here, and He will call us home as soon as it's done. We cannot waste any time. Our death will likely come with no warning. Be prepared every day."

She was prepared. She was prayerful. She lived a life of service, of gratitude, of laughter. I can think of no one who so personifies joy! From my prayer journal October 11, 2005:

"Betty Jo said to me today, 'After you die, your prayers remain.'"

> with gratitude to God
> for our friend,
> Laura

Father, daily You record Your love in our lives and on our hearts. Thank You for loving us with such hilarity through Betty Jo, and for all You taught us through her of prayer, of patience, of trust in You. We grin at Betty Jo's name and we pray in Jesus' name. Amen.

Do your best to present yourself to God as one . . .
who correctly handles the word of truth.

—2 TIMOTHY 2:15

18 FEBRUARY

Dear Friends,

The other day, as I was smarting over someone's insensitivity, a new thought came. It was as if God was saying to me, "OK. You're right about her. I've allowed you to experience this. I am confiding in you this truth: she is insensitive. Now, what are you going to do with this information? Will you handle it rightly?"

I had some choices, and I am practiced in every one. I could complain about her to others. Gossip. Pity her. Resent her. Avoid her. Luxuriate in the ridiculous notion that I am a superior creature. But here was a new idea—to regard this unpleasant truth about her as something that God was entrusting to me and allowing me to see for a reason. Would I recognize it as a call to pray for her? Would I treat it as an opportunity to invite God into her need? Would I work with Him in this or against Him? We don't typically recognize our observations about others as opportunities, but they are. The Lord is continuously alerting us to where He is needed and wants to be invited in.

God is able and willing to help in any way, in every circumstance, but He has instituted prayer as the means by which He will involve Himself in our affairs. He has given us free will. He has granted us a choice about inviting Him in or not and He will honor our decision. Almost a hundred years ago E.M. Bounds wrote, "It is only by prayer that God can help people. He who does not pray, therefore, robs himself of God's help and places God where He cannot help people."

When a thought comes to you ["that was a mean thing Jean did."] put a new spin on it and hit it right to God as you would a tennis ball. ["Lord, soften Jean's heart. May she yield to You. Forgive my resentment.] Another comes ["this cashier is so slow today!"] Send it soaring over the net to Him. ["She's tired, Lord. Strengthen her. Encourage her heart."] Another one comes. [Joe didn't thank me for what I did for him.] Hit it hard in His direction. [Help me do the right thing for the right reason. Thank You that You're with me. Thank You that You love me.]

Keep the rally going. How many bitter thoughts have we held onto and failed to send them flying? Keep hitting them to Him. How much time do we waste admiring our own tennis whites, our minds on how spotless we think we are? In the meantime, how many dead balls have accumulated at our feet? The ones we fail to hit over to Him will surely trip us up. Send them soaring.

He's eager to get into our game so let Him in on it. Send each thought to Him. As long as do so the score will remain Love-Love.

with you in Him,
Laura

Thank You for our life with You lived out in such bright light and fresh air. Thank You for our life with You laughing, reaching, running, waiting, playing, stretching, standing, serving. Amen.

. . . the one who feeds on me will live . . .

—JOHN 6:57

25 FEBRUARY

Dear Friends,

It is six weeks today since my mother-in-law's fall off a ladder and the start of her long recuperation. During those first hours in the Emergency Room never would I have anticipated the contentment and laughter and lessons that were ahead of me in days and evenings of feeding and nursing and playing Greek card games and hearing a lifetime of village tales.

I have learned 22 of her recipes in these weeks. In all the years since we met she has been cooking up a storm but I've rarely taken the time to stop and watch, listen or learn. I most often would wander in at the end of the day just in time to eat whatever she had prepared. (Don't we do this with God and prayer?) Busy, busy me, I would fit her in around more pressing commitments. I gave her my leftovers in terms of time, my less-than-full attention, not my freshest, best self. I valued what I did more than what she was doing.

I've been learning dishes out of a Greek cookbook for 25 years. And it turns out you can't learn it all from a book (either as a cook or as a Christian). The book helps, but you also have to watch. You have to stand side by side and do it together. You have to allow yourself to be corrected along the way. Without getting defensive. Without pretending to know it all. I've discovered that the opposite of a teachable spirit is that inner "No one's going to tell me what to do!!" that stomps to the fore at unlikely moments and has threatened to pollute some wonderful mornings together.

Dimitra urges on me her own mother's primary commandment: "Feed the family first! Every day that's your first order of business. Plan dinner. Get it started or made before anything else." And this always brings to my mind a line from Proverbs 31 on the godly wife. *She gets up while it is still dark; she provides food for her family* (v.15). I heard Jill Briscoe consider this verse as a description of our early morning time with the Lord. We feed on Him and fill up on Him so that we are able then to feed our family all day long. We make their spiritual wellbeing our priority by making sure we are spiritually nourished and fed and have something to share.

As Dimitra's bones are being knitted together our hearts are being knitted together. As her left hand heals, the other guides mine in forming meatballs for the soup, in measuring spices, in folding in the egg sauce.

Who is primary caregiver? Who is most healed? Who is the one feeding and who being fed? For whom has this recovery been the most fattening? I can answer only one with certainty.

> Grateful and growing,
> growing, growing,
> Laura

You who sent ravens to feed Elijah, and manna from heaven, You who filled Egypt's storehouses before the famine and cooked a hot breakfast for loved, mourning friends on the shore of a lake— Bread of Life, we praise Your name! We live on every word that proceeds out of your mouth. May we stop our foolish rushing and watch and listen and feast with You. Amen.

I lift up my eyes to the hills—where does my help come from?
My help comes from the LORD, the Maker of heaven and earth.

— PSALM 121:1-2

3 MARCH

Dear Friends,

I think God must take particular pleasure in orchestrating some of
His surprises—the creative ways by which He reminds us of His
power and presence.

A couple of years ago, when my son had to take a national li-
censing exam, he was unexpectedly assigned an immediate testing
date—only two days away—and in a city that was hours from
home. I drove him to the test site so he could review the material on
the way, and I spent the hours of his exam reading and praying in
the parking lot of a nondescript government building.

The exam went well, and on the drive home he told me about
his morning. Because of his late registration, every seat had been
taken in the usual testing room, so he and two others had been
placed in a separate, quieter room. Among other things, it was one
apparently used for worship services for the county jail because he
found his desk surrounded by the last thing he would have expected
under the circumstances—five large posters whose messages supplied just the composure and perspective he needed that day:

"You were created to be like Christ."

"You were formed for God's family."

"You were made for a mission."

"You were shaped for serving God."

"You were planned for God's pleasure."

Six months later my husband and I also found ourselves in an
unfamiliar city facing a test that had come sooner than expected.
We had flown into town that morning and sat now in an intensive

care waiting room preparing for what would be our final visit with my brother Nick, who was dying.

We talked quietly and prayed together, and as we lifted our heads, our eyes came to rest on a painting, a seascape, hanging on the wall. We looked at each other and smiled. This was a scene very familiar to us—a beautiful rendering of the beachside cliffs and park just down the road from our house, the site of scores of family walks, a place familiar and known and loved by us for fifteen years, and a sight all the more welcome for being so unexpected and unlikely in this sad, drab, anonymous room hundreds of miles from our city.

The painting, the posters, the prayers, all effected the same response—the same relief at the reminders of home, of who and Whose we are, of the fact that He goes before us even into those circumstances that rock our world and blow us off a predictable course. Ask Him this week to remind you of His presence with you and His great love for you. He delights to do so.

Love from Laura

We are anchored by every reminder and reassurance that You alone are God. Open our eyes and hearts to each one. Thank You that You are ever before us, preparing the way. Amen.

I will put breath in you, and you will come to life.
Then you will know that I am the LORD.

—EZEKIEL 37:6

10 MARCH

Dear Friends,

My mother-in-law is doing breathing exercises several times a day as part of her ongoing recovery. Using a little plastic device prescribed by her doctor, she breathes in as deeply as possible. Not only does this spirometer measure how much breath Dimitra is taking in, the deep breaths themselves exercise her lungs—an effective antidote to the shallow breathing that is the tendency with broken ribs. Expanding and filling her lungs prevents against tightening in her chest and pneumonia. We keep an eye on the numbers on the meter and have celebrated the steady increase in the volume of air she is able to take in.

Dimitra had been using the meter for weeks before I looked it over carefully and read the two words printed on its base: "Inspired volume." Who knew! All this time we have been measuring her inspiration! Breathing in is inhalation, also called inspiration. Both words mean the same thing—taking in the breath necessary for life. Dimitra's daily exercises fill her lungs and protect against losing her capacity for deep inspiration. What a perfect picture of what we are offered in prayer.

Prayer is not assigned spiritual homework but chosen time with a loved one, time during which we inspire Him, we take Him in, we breathe in the Breath of Life. In prayer time we fill up on His Word, His love. By so doing we protect ourselves against infection, against the congestion that otherwise threatens us. In time spent together, we expand our capacity for Him—His life in us and His teaching to us. The more we take in, the more we are given.

I grew up reciting this prayer in church: "Cleanse the thoughts of our hearts by the inspiration of thy Holy Spirit . . . " Spending time with God, inspiring His Spirit, we are cleansed of our meanness, our grumpiness, our irreverence. In His presence we are taught new ways of responding and reacting. We fill up on His truth. We are made more and more His.

The LORD God formed the man from the dust of the ground and breathed into his nostrils the breath of life, and the man became a living thing. (Genesis 2:7) God breathed out and we breathed in. He exhaled and we inhaled. He emptied Himself for us. We took Him in and we came to life. And that miracle is repeated every time we come to prayer, every time we sit with Him, every time we quiet ourselves to take in His word to us—we come to life, back to life, back to Him who is our life. Of all creation, only we humans are both material (dust of the ground) and spiritual (Gods' breath breathed into us). We alone have this capacity to commune with Him, to share our thoughts, hearts, fears with Him. To hear from Him, to know Him by His Word. We alone have this opportunity to live out our lives before Him and to be guided and corrected and steered along the way. As His we are offered prayer—a precious gift, capacity, opportunity we must not waste.

Hoping for hyperventilation!
Laura

Thank You for Your call to us, Your breath in us, Your gift to us. All praise to You, Lord Jesus Amen.

All the days ordained for me were written in your book
before one of them came to be.

—PSALM 139:16

17 MARCH

Dear Friends,

Long ago, I read a novel called *Body & Soul* that took my breath
away—the story of a musical prodigy who comes upon a piano at
the age of six and whose true life then begins. A masterfully written, memorable book.

Not long after that a birthday package arrived from my friend
Kathy. It was another copy of this great book. But before sending it,
Kathy had carried the book to the friend who lived next door and
had him inscribe it to me and add a birthday greeting. Her neighbor, Frank Conroy, just happened to be the book's author.

A book I had valued for its writing and story I now cherish even
more. It has been handled and inscribed to me by its author, a writer
I admire greatly. I was excited to know that Kathy had talked to
him about me, had told him how much I love his work. And she left
his house having secured something that I treasure—a volume that,
in addition to everything else, represents to me Kathy's caring and
friendship.

That same excitement I felt opening that book I felt again today
when a friend wrote to say that she is praying for me. She mentioned the retreat at which I am scheduled to speak in two weeks
(she remembered!) and said she is praying about it. She told me
specifically what she is asking God to do for me and for those who
attend. What a gift. What a friend.

How blithely we call over a shoulder, "I'll pray for you" as we
head on our way. How casually and unthinkingly we make and
receive this offer of something truly magnificent. Think about what

we are saying, offering, extending to our loved one when we say we will pray:

I am going to set aside other things to sit in the Lord's presence. I am going to go to Him on your behalf. I want to talk to Him about you. I want to tell Him about your need. I trust Him with it. I am going to place this care of yours into His hands and ask Him to inscribe it for you, to put His name on it. And because He knows me, He will do what I ask. He promises that. Your care will become His. And that care or concern will become something precious, something valuable, because He has touched it, because it has been in His hands. His name will be on it now.

Remember that He wrote this care into your life. He composed this situation long ago with you in mind, to show you His artistry, to touch your heart, to speak to you, to enrich you, to share with you something of Himself and His perspective. And I will carry this care of yours back to Him in prayer, acknowledging His authorship, seeking His hand upon it for you.

And then I am going to watch with great expectation and trust to see what He will do. I will trust Him in this even if you can't. If you can't lift your head to watch for what's coming, I will watch for you.

Cherish those friends who you know pray for you when they say they will. You can have no better friends than these. Be such a friend. Nothing can make you a better mother, son, spouse, grandparent, friend, than to be one who prays.

in Christ,
Laura

How slow we can be to deliver up our concerns to You, yet how easily, how willingly, You take them. You are ours, always ours, in every chapter, at every turn. Thank You, Lord. Amen.

Watch and pray so that you will not fall into temptation.

— MATTHEW 26:40

24 MARCH

Dear Friends,

I've often read the accounts in Matthew and Mark of the disciples sleeping when Christ needed them most. In Gethsemane He needed their companionship and asked them to be praying with Him. Instead, they slept. This week I noticed a telling detail in Luke's account. *When he rose from prayer and went back to the disciples, he found them asleep, exhausted from sorrow.* (Luke 22:45). Exhausted from sorrow.

In 1Samuel 30, when King David and his men return to their camp after an absence, they find that their enemies have not only attacked and burned the camp but have also taken captive all of their wives and children. *So David and his men wept aloud until they had no strength left to weep.* (v. 4) Sometime later, when they set out to pursue the enemy, a third of them had to stay behind for *two hundred men were too exhausted to cross the ravine.* (v. 10) Too exhausted from weeping. Too exhausted from grief.

When we are overwhelmed by circumstances, we are not inclined to be battling our twin enemies of despair and disbelief. The temptation that most threatens us at such a time is the temptation to doubt God, to question His goodness. When we most need to be reminded of God's presence and power and love, we may be least likely to be praying. Christ, Himself overwhelmed with sorrow in Gethsemane, (Mark 14:34) urged His disciples to pray because He needed it, but also because He knew how much they did. What they most needed at such a time could come to them from God alone. What we most need can come to us only from Him.

When David and those who fought with him were successful against the enemy and returned triumphant, the victors were not inclined to share the spoils with those who had stayed behind grief-stricken. But David prevailed. He pointed out that the victory had been given by God Himself and David decreed that *The share of the man who stayed with the supplies is to be the same as that of him who went down to the battle. All will share alike.* (v. 24) Incredibly, God's power and presence and love are as much ours when we are spiritually inactive or exhausted from sorrow as when we shine for Him. They are neither earned by us nor owed to us but are His gifts—rewards of being His.

Jesus offered remarkable assurance of this after the disciples failed Him in the Garden. *Rise! Let us go!* He said upon finding them asleep yet again (Mark 14:42). Whether you have done what I asked or have failed, you are Mine. Stay with Me. Don't linger back here in regret. *Rise! Let us go!* Together. You are Mine and I want you with Me. Work remains to be done and I want you with Me in it.

Prayer is God's great gift—the means by which He conveys to us all that we most need. Let nothing keep us from it. When overwhelmed by sorrows, in the face of temptations to doubt or to substitute other comforts or remedies, run to Him, run to prayer.

with you there,
Laura

You whose arms are always open, eager, eager for us with You—we come with gladness. Amen.

I will fear no evil, for you are with me . . .

—PSALM 23:4

31 MARCH

Dear Friends,

On our morning walks these days, my mother-in-law and I see the same sad scene played out too often. Kids walking to the nearby elementary school, scuffing along in silence, kicking at pebbles, head down, while mom strides a few steps ahead or behind, animatedly talking on her cell phone.

What riches to walk to school and home again hand-in-hand with a parent. And add to that picture the luxury of a relaxed pace and conversation. In the midst of a challenging lesson or exam, imagine looking out the classroom window to see that loved face, an encouraging smile. When my cousin Carol was very young, and feeling homesick during long school days, her mother took a job for one hour each day in the school cafeteria. At noon, the lunch lady who served Carol her lunch was her own loved, smiling mother.

If we look out the classroom window during a challenge we won't see the Lord there smiling at us. He is not as distant as that. He is beside us at our desk. And on every walk, to and from every challenge and celebration, He is alongside, His hand extended. And He is always the One closest to the road as we walk—between us and any threat coming our way.

We like to pretend ours is a solo trek, and too often we're not mindful of our sweet Companion. We forge ahead of Him or lag behind. We choose our route and choose to forget His presence, His willingness, His eagerness to guide, to guard, to feed, to answer us.

His is the Word of leading we most need, but so often our walk is taken up in chatter with others. We could be talking with Him, but we content ourselves with talking about Him.

Better than anyone, He knows the lay of the land. Yet we veer from His side to scramble unnecessarily over hills and past bushes that snag our clothes and scratch our legs. Looking down to avoid the undergrowth that impedes our chosen way, our heads aren't up to see Him beckoning us to His easier path, the one He has cleared for us.

Stop. Look. Listen. Where is He standing, waiting for you to rejoin Him? Go. Go to Him in prayer. Hand over your heavy book bag. Tell Him about your day. Take His hand and let Him walk you home.

loved, led,
Laura

For Your patience when we go our own way, thank You. For Your eagerness to walk with us. That You are waiting for us at every crossing. That we are not alone in all this, are not without a loving guide—

Father and Friend, You free us from snares. Thank You for Your leading, Your love, the feel of Your hand in ours. Amen.

*. . . and everyone who was willing and whose heart moved him
came and brought an offering to the Lord . . .*

— EXODUS 35:21

7 APRIL

Dear Friends,

Years ago on a ski trip in Colorado, my family was given a wonderful gift. Pete was a teenager at the time and spent the days of that
trip with friends, as did my husband and I. One day before lunch,
hours before we were to meet up with him, Pete fell and broke his
wrist. His name was not posted on any of the ski lift message boards
we passed that day, and our cell phones were inaudible as we skied.
So by the time we learned what had happened, hours had passed.

In the meantime Karen, the mother of one of Pete's classmates
and a stranger to all of us until that day, had taken him to the hospital. Until we arrived and gave our permission, he could not be
given so much as an aspirin, so he had spent several painful hours
waiting to be treated. And Karen had waited with him. She had
been cheerful, diverting company as they spent hours talking together. By the time we joined them, a friendship had been born.

And it was a friendship that was to last. In the years afterward,
when the two attended the same sports events at school, they often
sat together in the bleachers. Karen was one of the honored few
adults Pete invited to his eighteenth birthday party. By graduation
time, Karen's daughter made an amused reference to the friendship
in their high school yearbook.

At the hospital, Karen gave to Peter her most precious commod-
ity—her time. She surrendered her will for the day, her plans and
desires, and gave her day over to Peter. And she did so without
displaying the slightest trace of resentment or longing for what she
was missing on the slopes with her own family. She gave willingly
and with a cheerful heart. What an impression that made on our

son! What an impression it made on all of us. By her sacrifice she embodied so many of the things we had tried (with mere words) to convey to Peter over the years—what giving really means and friendship and selflessness.

A solid relationship can develop in only one way—by investing time in getting to know one another. And a solid relationship with God is no exception. When we choose to spend time alone with Him in prayer, it is a sacrifice. We forsake other things to do this, we miss out on other things to do this. And that's why the gift is so precious to Him and so richly rewarded. We are offering that which is hardest for us to part with—our time.

He has given a choice in this so we come to prayer of our own free will. That makes prayer a freewill offering of the finest kind. We are willingly yielding this bit of time—and our plans for it and our desires for it and anything we might accomplish in it—and in so doing we are demonstrating and living out what we so often claim with mere words—"knowing You matters to me. What You want matters to me. I am Yours. My time is Yours."

with you in Him,
Laura

Lord God, may each of my days be one of listening and yielding myself to You so that Your perfect will can be done for me and through me. For the sake of Your honor and glory. Amen.

No eye has seen, no ear has heard, no mind has conceived
what God has prepared for those who love him . . .

— 1 CORINTHIANS 2:9

14 APRIL

Dear Friends,

Three years ago I spent a few memorable days alone in London, mostly in museums. My favorite, the Victoria and Albert, is the world's largest museum of decorative arts. It is filled with silver and toys, gowns, furniture, needlework and sculpture.

The biggest surprise of the trip was how it felt to go through a museum by myself.

I had never realized what a difference the presence or absence of companions make in the experience. Alongside friends, I often am directing their attention—"Wow! Look at that!"—or am slowing or speeding up my pace to accommodate theirs. Until I was alone I had never noticed how much I talk my way through experiences, keeping up a running commentary of my reactions and soliciting theirs. "That's gorgeous! Do you like that? I've never heard of him. Which one is your favorite?" In the company of others my attention splays out in every horizontal direction with one eye and only a part of my mind on the art while the rest of me keeps constant tabs on everyone else and whether or not they seem to be taken care of. "Do you want to sit? Are you enjoying this?" I wonder if I'm talking too much . . .

Alone, the experience was very different. I had the luxury of setting my own pace. I ventured anywhere I wanted. I followed my own preferences and lingered at favorite spots. I took the time to consider what I was looking at. I was silent; the experience was not diluted by chatter. I rediscovered that I could actually form and hold an opinion all by myself without requiring anyone to second the motion. I did miss sharing the experience at times, particularly when I saw something spectacular. I had to turn to a complete stranger a time or two to demand, "Isn't that gorgeous?!"

By prayer we daily make our way through the great treasure house of being His, marveling at the shine and glorious workmanship of what we find there. We go alone or in the company of others, and both trips are vital. Today my husband and I prayed together over a shared concern and ever since then my heart has been relieved and at peace in a way it had not been before, despite weeks of praying over this on my own. There is power in joining our voice with another, in approaching God hand in hand with someone else. Both the experience of offering it to God and the prayer itself are magnified in being shared. *For where two or three come together in my name, there am I with them.* (Matthew 18:20)

But solitary prayer is required as well and offers rewards of its own. *But when you pray, go into your room, close the door and pray to Your Father, who is unseen.* (Matthew 6:6) Silent, we hear and see things we would otherwise miss. Alone with Him we linger where we need to and confide the secret things. And He does the same. Our gift to Him of undivided attention is reciprocated with fresh displays of His loving character, new exhibits of who we are in Christ.

Isn't it gorgeous?!

Laura

Thank You for Your eagerness as You await us in prayer, and Your joy at our appearing. Amen.

Fix these words of mine in your hearts and minds . . .

—DEUTERONOMY 11:18

21 APRIL

Dear Friends,

Years ago, at a family party, a loved one I had not seen in years surprised me with a gift. "I have something for you," Linda said as she handed me a small lidded basket.

It was filled with dried leaves and flowers, withered and darkened with age. 'Herbs?' I wondered. 'Potpourri?' I sniffed but there was no aroma. "Thank you," I said, a bit hesitant. She smiled and nodded. "Read the card."

In an instant something ordinary became the most personal and significant of gifts. What a difference three words can make! That day the words were these: "Your wedding bouquet!"

After Linda's friend Carol had caught my wedding bouquet more than two decades earlier, Linda had preserved the flowers and presented them to me now.

What a difference three words can make! Preserved for us, presented to us by a Loved One, today and always the words are these:

I chose you	*learn from me*
love the Lord	*You are mine*
take heart, daughter	*be my help*
Jesus is Lord	*You have delivered*
He will defend	*just and true*
It is written	*but God will*
Son of God	*children of God*
I am willing	*He is risen*
but I trust	*King of kings*

take and eat
pray with me
listen and understand
Come, Lord Jesus
don't be afraid
Faithful and True
Lord God Almighty
take my yoke
feed my sheep
trust in God
Abraham believed God
I am gentle
Word of God
the Holy One
Lazarus, come out!
Who touched me?
it is I
Behold, I knock
prayer to heaven
the Lord lives!
I will sing
my heart trusts
but rejoicing comes
enthroned as King
remain in me

Praise our God
Go and tell
come, follow me
Quiet! Be still
I am thirsty
repent and believe
bore our sins
I am He
It is finished
Come to me
Jesus was born
grace and peace
serve Him only
Your kingdom come
do not judge
Do you believe
Love one another
I desire mercy
rock of refuge
the Lord heard
in your hands
Father, forgive them
Lamb of God
I will praise
peace I give

Laura

Loving, living Word! We are forgiven! We are Yours! Receive our
praise! Amen and amen.

So then, it was not you who sent me here, but God.

— GENESIS 45:8

28 APRIL

Dear Friends,

I woke with a start this morning at 4:00 with a scrap of a verse running through my mind, *"consider your ways."* I started to pray for a
loved one. "Yes, Lord, please make sure they do consider their ways.
That's a good way to put it. They really need to think about what
they're doing, the choices they're making." I rolled over and waited
for sleep . . . I waited some more . . .

Consider your ways. Wait. You mean me? Is this about me? Of
course this was about me. I have had a bug coming on all weekend.
No sniffles or illness, but a little germ of resentment has been perco-
lating and threatening to break out all over in a scarlet fever of
angry words and finger pointing.

I have a good case—any of my faithful friends would agree. It's
not fair. It's too much. I've gone the extra mile. I've been more than
reasonable. I've done my share. I've yielded like crazy. I've been
patient, accommodating, loving. Enough already!

But God . . . That's the little phrase that tripped me up all day
today and kept me from calling a friend for sympathy and back up.
But God likely sees things differently. What would He say if I called
Him for sympathy and back up?

This evening I tried it. I went to my prayer place to rant and cry.
I hated hearing the words, the ugly sound of my resentments articu-
lated and listed. Is this what it means to confess? Why don't I feel
any better? My focus stayed locked on me vs. them. I kept building
my case.

But God . . . I quieted myself. Blaming the people involved and
listing my grievances, I stayed angry and defensive. But did these
human agents of my misery initiate the situation? Is my battle with

them or is it with Him who controls all things? If I believe God is sovereign, as I claim to, I have to acknowledge that this situation has come into my life by His hand, for His purposes. This has come to me from Him—Him whom I know to be loving and not capricious. Trustworthy. I looked past the human relationships and rested my eyes, my thoughts, on Him. My tone changed.

Nothing leads us so resolutely to prayer as the recognition of God's hand behind life events, and of His power alone to affect, to heal, to solve, to clarify, to fix, to change them. We spend so much time in line at the Complaints Department when we could step right into the presence of the One with all the power to enact any correction necessary.

In Psalm 51 David begs divine mercy and forgiveness and restoration on the basis of God's unfailing love and great compassion—exactly the basis upon which we can approach Him as well. Over and over and all our lives. As many times as necessary. And the greatest evidence of His Spirit at work in us will be not only our willingness to acknowledge our sin but also the quickness with which we hand it over and then accept His forgiveness.

failing and forgiven,
Laura

Heavenly Father, even when I don't understand what You're trying to do, may it go Your way. May I work with You, not against You. Thank You for showing me my sin. What a relief is the truth. And thank You for forgiving me. In Jesus' name. Amen

Praise be to the God and Father of our Lord Jesus Christ,
the Father of all compassion and the God of all comfort,
who comforts us in all our troubles, so that we can comfort those
in any trouble with the comfort we ourselves have received from God.

— 2 Corinthians 1:4

5 May

Dear Friends,

When my dad died twenty years ago this month, I received a number of sympathy cards and notes. Among them was a particularly beautiful letter of consolation from Ann, a contemporary and long-time friend of my parents and a wonderful friend to me.

Six years later Ann herself died very unexpectedly. The loss was stunning and felt to me like the last straw in a series of losses. I couldn't quite believe God would allow it. Ann had been the one who stepped in with just the word I needed when my mother died, when my father died, when my brother Jess died. I couldn't forgive God for this one, and I kept my distance from Him for days. I avoided prayer and slammed through my daily tasks. I remember the angry thoughts that eventually became angry prayers, "You could have saved her! You could have kept her alive. She died because it was Your timing. I can't believe You allowed this."

But I see now that shooting off those angry words to God and even my initial avoidance of prayer were evidences, oddly enough, of my faith. Both were fueled by my recognition that this death could only have happened by His permissive will.

Taking our anger to God in prayer is just the thing to do. It is an acknowledgement of His Lordship over the circumstances, and every such acknowledgement honors Him. Going to prayer in our anger is evidence that spiritually we have our eyes in the right place, even if those eyes are glaring in protest. We take our angry selves to Him, to prayer, because He is the One to whom we must confess both the anger and the defiance behind it—that spirit in us that demands that things go our way. He is the only One who can forgive and relieve us of both, and He is waiting and most willing to do so. Because after the angry prayers the other prayers can come—the deeper prayers of the heart, the hurting heart. Bringing all of it to Him perfectly positions us to receive His most personal comfort.

For me that comfort came in a most unlikely form. Soon after Ann's death I nearly slipped on a piece of paper on my kitchen floor one day. I picked it up only to discover that it was the letter Ann had written to me when my father had died. The letter must have been in a kitchen drawer, perhaps stuck to something I had handled earlier in the day. I had not seen it in six years. This perfect consolation had been written for me years earlier by Ann herself and was delivered to me now a second time by the God who loves me.

I copied the letter and passed it along to Ann's two sons, for God's comfort is given to be shared. In those days just after her death, imagine them receiving, in their mother's own words and handwriting, gentle instruction on how to bear the loss of a loved parent. Tender shepherd, indeed.

His with you,

Laura

Comforter, Companion, Convicter and Victor, we praise You as Father, Friend and King. Amen

Walk about Zion, go around her, count her towers,
consider well her ramparts, view her citadels, and tell of them
to the next generation. For this God is our God
for ever and ever; he will be our guide even to the end.

—PSALM 48:12-14

12 MAY

Dear Friends,

So often when I visited my brother Nick in the hospital, he had a certain book within easy reach. It was obvious from its well-worn condition that this was a volume Nick opened daily and more than daily—the cover was coming loose, the page corners were curled. More than almost anything, the image of that tattered book represents Nick to me and his determination to understand things and to make sense of the world.

The book was a dictionary. That falling-apart dictionary declared the fact that Nick would not settle for reading a novel or the newspaper or even watching TV without taking the time to consider exactly what he was reading or being told. He wanted to know. He actively sought to apprehend. He particularly wanted to fully grasp every word he read in the Bible. He wanted to live out his trust in God in practical decisions and choices, and he wanted to do so fully informed about what was being promised, commanded, declared and requested of him. He didn't want to miss a thing.

As children we know every inch of the yard where we play and explore day by day. Years later we walk around and around our first car, a new house, taking in every detail. We know the face of our sweetheart better than we know our own. We examine every toe and dimple of the newborn placed in our arms. And yet too often we are content to leave unexplored our great inheritance as children of God.

We have entered into a rich estate and have full possession of it right here, right now. Studying His Word is a vital part of coming to know all that is ours as His. The coming of summer also offers a chance to venture out and to walk the land with our children, to explore the mansion itself, to try out the tools we have been given, to taste the contents of every pot in the kitchen. God asks us to dig deeply into His Word but also to live out our faith—to entrust to Him our loved ones and our cares, to test Him in His promises, to take His hand, to serve, to come away with Him by ourselves to a quiet spot, to stop being afraid, to watch for Him at work all around us.

This life with Him is not to be a static, studious thing but active and practical and fruitful. He offers to relieve us of our self focus and to give us new eyes to see and a more far-reaching perspective. He wants to live in us and to love through us. May we not miss a bit of the blessing and bounty that are ours as His.

Happy Summer!
Laura

Thank You, Father, for Your power and presence and patience. For your grace and good gifts. May all of Your loving will be done by us and for us and in us and through us. For Your honor, for our joy, and in Christ's name. Amen.

. . .

Year Four

. . .

Love your neighbor . . .

LEVITICUS 19:18, MATTHEW 19:19, MATTHEW 22:39,
MARK 12:31, MARK 12:33, LUKE 10:27,
ROMANS 13:9, GALATIONS 5:14, JAMES 2:8

8 SEPTEMBER

Dear Friends,

At a red light recently, as I held out money to a homeless man, he surprised me by announcing as he approached, "My name is James." In that quick interval before the light turned green he reached for the money in my outstretched hand, but even more eagerly for the hand itself, for a human connection. *I'm a person. Wait before you zoom away—I have a name. I want to be known.*

Several houses down our street lives a little girl. I have only ever known her by the sound of her voice. She is usually playing outside and she is usually screaming. That seems to be the way she relieves tension and declares herself to a world too busy for her. Bloodcurdling screams as she rides her bike, as she chases her brother, as she waits for her parents to get home from work. Sometimes I pray for her. Other times I resent her interrupting my work. I sit in my office angrily clenching my jaw as I write about the love of God.

Yesterday, when I returned home from a walk, she was playing in front of my house. Face to face for the first time with this tiny creature, and she spoke in a quiet voice, almost accusing, "Do you know my name?"

I was taken aback by the question and ashamed to realize I did not know her name. "It's Gabriella," she informed me. *You pray for me from afar. Do you even know who I am? Would you spare any of your precious time for me?*

Sometimes I go through the Christian motions forgetting the point. I rush past the needy people in my path on my way to serving

God in a larger or 'official' capacity. My eye is on the far horizon, on my 'important' duties while a child is lonely at my feet.

As Christians we gear up for the grand gesture while over and over He asks that we love one another. I was surprised to discover how often *"Love your neighbor"* is repeated in the Bible. Christ asks us to slow down and regard the person in front of us, to look them in the eye, to find out their name, who they are, what they need. He asks us to listen. C.S. Lewis said, "The rule for all of us is perfectly simple. Do not waste time bothering whether you 'love' your neighbor; act as if you did."

This is the real and immediate assignment for every one of us— to live out the love of Christ moment by moment, in our backyard, in a ballroom, in a sanctuary, on a soccer field and street corner. One cup of cold water at a time.

In His love,
Laura

Father, may we make You visible, make You known to those around us. May we serve Your purposes in this world. For Your honor. Amen.

Those who look to him are radiant; their faces are
never covered with shame.

—Psalm 34:5

15 September

Dear Friends,

Yesterday some things came to mind that I needed to confess and I did so. I confessed them and even thanked God for pointing them out to me. And that was that. But was it? It seemed too easy. I didn't seem to felt guilty enough, and I started to second-guess myself. Was I truly repentant? What does it mean to "repent" anyway? I looked up the word and was surprised to discover that the primary definition does not mention feelings at all. To repent is "to turn from sin and dedicate oneself to the amendment of one's life." God does want our sin to grieve us as it does Him but repentance, first and foremost, is a decisive action, not an emotional response.

Brother Lawrence, who lived in the 1600s, was greatly admired for his faithfulness to God. A friend reports that Brother Lawrence responded to his sin this way, "…when he had failed in his duty, he only confessed his fault, saying to God, 'I shall never do otherwise if You leave me to myself; it is You who must hinder my falling and mend what is amiss' . . .after this he gave himself no uneasiness about it."

How simple and honest his response seems to me. He "only confessed" his fault. No agonizing, no excuses. He freely admitted that his inclination was toward sin and did not fool or flatter himself into believing otherwise. He recognized and acknowledged God as his only hope against sin. Best of all, after confession "he gave himself no uneasiness about it." How refreshing I find that last! Forgiven, and the incident is forgotten. I tend to hang back at the self-focused place called regret. Am I trying to prove my remorse to God by berating myself? I express amazement that I could do such a thing as sin, but why does it surprise me? Who do I think I am? Brother Lawrence takes it for granted that he will sin. Of course he will. Of course we will.

Sometimes my confession is delayed as I struggle to find words adequate to convey my regret. I strain for convincing evidence of my remorse. And in the meantime God waits, unimpressed. He does not require elaborate wording. He seeks humble acknowledgement and simple agreement. He is ready to move on long before I am.

Brother Lawrence asked forgiveness and moved on with God. He did not give in to the temptation to beat himself up or even to think about himself. He kept his eyes on God and his foot in step with God's. Says he, "I besought His pardon, and without losing heart I set my spirit right, and returned anew into His presence, as though I had never wandered from Him."

How encouraging is this example that comes down to us through hundreds of years—not allowing himself to be slowed or diverted by despair or self-analysis, Brother Lawrence quickly, decisively, got himself back where he belonged—right with God.

with you in Christ,
Laura

Father, may I regard myself in honest terms not considering myself better or worse than I am. May my confession be offered plainly, humbly, honestly, frequently. For Your glory. Amen.

Give thanks to the LORD, for he is good. His love endures forever . . .
to the One who remembered us in our low estate
His love endures forever. And freed us from our enemies,
His love endures forever. And who gives food to every creature.
His love endures forever.
Give thanks to the God of heaven. His love endures forever.

—PSALM 136:1-4, 23-26

22 SEPTEMBER

Dear Friends,

My friend had an important and potentially upsetting meeting with a lawyer last week, a meeting she nervously had awaited many weeks. The appointment time was 8:30 on a Tuesday morning. On Monday, when we spoke, I assured her that I would be praying.

I didn't sleep well that night and when my eyes flew open on Tuesday morning I looked at the clock first thing and saw that it was exactly at 8:30. God is faithful! I jumped out of bed and started to pray for my friend. When I next looked up it was 9:01, and I hurried downstairs to make breakfast for my family before I had to be somewhere.

I called my friend that afternoon to see how things had gone. All went well, she said, except that half an hour into their meeting the lawyer had unexpectedly been called away. They would have to meet again because their meeting had ended so abruptly. "That's because my family needed breakfast!" I told her, and we laughed.

Both of us took the whole experience as a wonderful assurance of how involved God is with the details of our lives and how much He wants us to be entrusting our concerns to Him in prayer. And when we are faithful to pray He will be faithful to respond.

Why was I surprised by His waking me up at the perfect moment? Why do reminders of His power and sovereignty and love and involvement in the small details of my life surprise me? This morning I apologized to Him that they do. Because my surprise is evidence of something I am sorry about—too often I pray without real certainty that He is listening or that my prayers will make a difference. Too often I pray because I know I should and because it makes me feel better. But I want to pray Believing! I want to pray remembering that I am engaged in conversation with the Creator of the universe, that I am there at prayer at His invitation! When we talk, He is fully focused and is able and willing and sure to involve Himself in the circumstances of my life or whichever life I am lifting to Him in prayer.

He will be faithful to do His part. May I be faithful to do mine—may I pray. The details of the dramas and challenges and worries of our lives change, but He does not change. His character does not change. His promises do not change. And prayer is, unchangingly, the answer. Whatever the question. His answer, His calm, His solution is only a prayer away.

Praying with you,
Laura

Lord, we praise You as unchanging and faithful. Thank You! And for this gift of prayer. Amen.

I pray also that the eyes of your heart may be enlightened
in order that you may know the hope to which he has called you,
the riches of his glorious inheritance in the saints,
and his incomparably great power for us who believe.

— EPHESIANS 1:18

29 SEPTEMBER

Dear Friends,

In 2 Samuel 24, King David ordered that a census be taken of his troops—a seemingly innocent, even wise move for a commander. *"Go throughout the tribes of Israel from Dan to Beersheba and enroll the fighting men, so that I may know how many there are."*

It was only after the numbers had been reported to him that David was conscience-stricken and confessed to the Lord what he now recognized as sin. What was his sin? It was self-sufficiency, trusting in numbers, believing that the strength of his kingdom derived from the number of fighting men rather than the presence and grace of God.

What numbers do I trust in? What figures do I misuse to estimate my worth in this world? What measures represent my value? The number on the scale this morning, certainly. My son's SAT scores or GPA. My blood pressure, blood counts, bank balance. 911. The number of wedding anniversaries reached or the number of times I've read through the Bible. 127 is a number I rely on—that's the cookbook page number of my never-fail tetrazzini recipe. I might tally the number of exotic vacations taken or degrees earned. How many friends turn to me in a crisis? What's the number of laps I swam today? My dress size. My zip code. How is it that I, who know the Lord and know how He loves and values me, measure my worth as a person by how many fat grams I've eaten? Or the number of birthday cards or calls that come in?

The problems come with horizontal thinking. When I stop

looking up and start looking around me, trouble starts. When I compare myself to my neighbor, my perspective gets skewed. It is significant, I think, that the most common prayer position in the Bible is head up, eyes open, looking to the Lord for what is needed. That needs to be our position also. Not looking down in despair or looking around to compare what we have with what our neighbor has. Not looking behind to see where we were yesterday or what we used to have. Not looking ahead to what we think we're owed. No, but looking up to who God is and to who we are as His.

So much that I have now I will not retain. So little of it is lasting or as important as I tend to think. We dishonor God by misplaced trust and by valuing things that He does not. We sing rightly with the hymn, "My hope is based on nothing less than Jesus' blood and righteousness. I dare not trust the sweetest frame, but wholly lean on Jesus' name. On Christ the solid rock I stand—all other ground is sinking sand."

In prayer we are realigned, our eyes are lifted from this world and our limitations. Our strength and security are with Him, in Him.

> Strong, with you,
> Laura

All that I have is from You. All that I need is mine in You. May I never look elsewhere. Amen

Now may the Lord's strength be displayed . . .

—NUMBERS 14:17

6 OCTOBER

Dear Friends,

Last Friday I happened to receive two different emails that mentioned Caleb and the scouts sent into the Promised Land. That day I also unexpectedly had a visit with a real-life, three-year-old Caleb, one of my favorite people. I decided that evening to reread Numbers 13-14 to see if the Lord wanted to say something to me through Caleb's story.

Twelve men—one from each tribe of Israel—were sent by the Lord ahead of the Israelites into the Promised Land. They were to explore and to see what the people and land and crops were like and to report back on what they found. Moses urged them also to try to bring back some of the fruit of the land.

For forty days the men explored, and when they returned to Moses and the people this was their report: *"Yes, the land does flow with milk and honey! But . . . "* And they went on to describe the big, fearsome inhabitants of the land. Verse 32 says They spread among the Israelites a bad report about the land they had explored and the result throughout the camp was crippled faith, crying, raised voices, rebellion, resentment and contempt toward God.

Of the twelve scouts, only Caleb and Joshua were excited by what they had seen and confident, grateful, and faithful in their report. *"The land we passed through and explored is exceedingly good, they said"* (Numbers 14:7). They urged against faithlessness, grumbling and fear.

The Lord's warning to me through this story was clear and forceful. Those of us who have been led to faith in Christ have stepped into a blessed land that many know nothing about. We live with a conscious awareness of God's presence with us and His power, love and forgiveness. And in this sense we are walking ahead of the many people who will eventually come to faith but are not yet there. What sort of report are we sending back from the land of Christ? Is it a good report? Intentionally or not we are influencing others' perceptions of God. And that is a privilege we must handle responsibly and with great care. How He is portrayed and represented is a matter of grave importance to the Lord.

What are we conveying of Christ by our responses, our attitudes and anxieties, our cheerfulness, trust, confidence, consistency? Every complaint or expression of dissatisfaction is an accusation against God. I slander Him with my grumbling and negativity because it suggests that He is unloving or prone to mistakes.

Would anyone looking at my life and responses surmise that life with Christ makes a difference? What sort of fruit of the Promised Land is on display in my life? For the honor of God's name, may we never "spread a bad report" among the people about the glorious land we daily explore.

grateful girl scout,
Laura

Holy, loving Father, thank You for the incomparable relief and joy of walking this earth hand-in-hand with You and in Your strength and love. We are Yours! May our lives reflect that glorious truth and cause others to look to You with hope. We live and pray as Yours, in Christ. Amen.

. . . to you, O Lord, I lift up my soul.

—Psalm 86:4

13 October

Dear Friends,

Each of my parents had a possession or two that they particularly valued. My mother wore a jade ring that had been her mother's. My father loved music and prized his record collection. Both of them loved books. But the item that comes immediately to mind when I think of family treasures is a blue plastic cereal bowl that sat on my mother's dresser as far back as I can remember. It held the curls from an early haircut of her youngest child, my brother Toby.

We were not a particularly disciplined bunch (thank you, Dr. Spock) and were perpetually in and out of her room and cupboards. But that bowl was one thing that we knew was not to be disturbed. Even at the age of five or six I was not too young to note and be touched by how sentimentally she treasured and guarded those curls.

My mother-in-law has had a crystal bowl on her kitchen table since her wedding over fifty years ago. It is one of the first things you see as you come into the apartment and the last as you leave, so that bowl has long been the spot where important mail is left—either incoming or outgoing—or the fruit or treats that looked particularly good that day at the market. Checking the contents of that bowl as you come in or head out is a wise move and often yields something unexpected and delicious.

Our Father's bowls described in Revelation are neither plastic nor crystal, but golden. And they hold what is most precious to Him—*golden bowls full of incense, which are the prayers of the saints.* (Revelation 5:8) There are our outcries, our conversation, our questions and praises and thanks—the various ways we share with Him our lives here on earth. Those prayers are to Him aromatic and valuable, but they are also holy. They are held up in golden bowls to Him who is pure and who cannot be in the presence of anything unclean or unholy. So those prayers are pure in His sight and wholly acceptable. As are we.

Prayer is our gift, the means by which we invite Him in wherever we are wrestling or celebrating or questioning. Prayer releases His power into the situation and launches us into an entirely different arena. We are freed of the weight, the worry, the responsibility and we become instead awed spectators of His power and glory.

Keep in mind the royal reception your prayers will get upon arrival. Consider them as precious and valuable as He does, and treat them accordingly. Give your prayers a royal send-off. Stop whatever else you are doing and take care with your words and tone. You are sending a message into the throne room of the King—a King eagerly awaiting it, loved child.

Laura

We come again to You, Father, with our prayers, and with what delight and attentive care you receive them. We come to say thank You. We speak to You, we pray to You, in Jesus' name. Amen.

When the wine was gone, Jesus' mother said to him,
"They have no more wine."

— JOHN 2:3

20 OCTOBER

Dear Friends,

How diligently and earnestly we have been praying in recent months for friends and family members in need. Last night I opened my Bible for too brief a moment before sleeping but even in only two short verses I saw a wonderful picture of prayer and why we pray and what is being accomplished when we do.

After teaching in the synagogue, Jesus and some of his disciples went over to Simon (Peter's) house. Simon's mother-in-law was in bed with a fever, and they told Jesus about her. So he went to her, took her hand and helped her up. The fever left her and she began to wait on them. (Mark 1:30-31).

The disciples were aware of her illness and they told Jesus about her. When we have a loved one in need, we tell Jesus about them. Prayer is simply that. "Lord, my neighbor, Joan, is ill." In response to what we tell Him, Jesus

— goes to her

— takes her hand

— helps her up.

When you pray for your ailing friend, Jesus goes to her and takes her hand. Isn't that a lovely picture? He helps her up. He may lift her from her bed or He may lift her eyes from her circumstances. He helps her. He is there and on the case because you told Him about her. Your prayer has invited Him in.

It says Jesus took her hand and helped her up and her fever departed. Jesus entered and her fever departed. Like everything and everyone on earth, illness is subject to the Lordship of Christ. He reigns over it. Fever remains or flees according to His will and plan.

In either case, we can trust Him. He is sovereign and accomplishing His eternal, loving purpose.

Our part as pray-ers is to entrust to Him those whom we know are in need. And the larger result? Simon's mother-in-law got up and began to serve Jesus and His disciples. A laborer has been added to the kingdom. A word to Jesus sends Him to her and He frees her to serve Him. By prayer we take part in expanding God's kingdom on earth.

Prayer can be as simple as this—reporting to Jesus our friend's need. He knows already, of course. But by turning to Him in prayer we are acknowledging His Lordship over this situation. We are demonstrating and re-stating and living out our faith in Him. And on the basis of our trust, He will approach our needy friend where she lies and do what only He can do. It begins with prayer. It begins with this: they told Jesus about her.

in Christ,
Laura

Lord, sometimes we strain to do more in prayer than You are asking us to. May we simply and continually convey into Your hands our loved ones and our concerns. We trust You. Amen.

*But from everlasting to everlasting the LORD's love is with those who
fear him, and his righteousness with their children's children . . .*

— PSALM 103:17

27 OCTOBER

Dear Friends,

Several months ago I wrote a letter to a young friend who was about
to marry. Among other things I said this: "Your mother prays for
you faithfully, often, specifically, and with trust. So does your father.
I also pray for you and so do others. To be prayed for is great riches.
And by that measure you and [your fiancé] are very rich. You have
generations behind you of believing, God-honoring relatives. That
is also great riches. Many of the blessings you are enjoying now are
the fruit of the faithfulness of your grandparents and their prede-
cessors who lived long before you were born. And, similarly, your
children and grandchildren and far-future generations will be
blessed by the choices you make now and the faithfulness you live
out."

Weeks later those words were confirmed in my own life in a
thrilling way when I read for the first time some family documents
of which I have copies. The most remarkable is a family history
written in the 1720s by my great-great- (eight "greats") grandfather
for his children and their descendants. He begins by telling of the
life and faith of his own great-grandfather born in 1500! This is
how the memoir begins: "My dear children,

"Having observed the deep interest you have taken in all that
has befallen your ancestors, . . . I am induced to write down their
history for your use, to the end that the pious examples of those
from whom we derive our origin may not be lost to you, or those
who succeed you.

"I trust that it may be the means of engaging you to dedicate
yourselves wholly and unreservedly to the service of God whom

they worshipped at the risk of their lives, and to be steadfast in the profession of that pure faith for which they suffered the severest hardships with unshaken constancy. And also that you may admire the watchful and wonderful providences God exerted in supporting and preserving them through every trial. Indeed, without looking beyond the compass of your own memories, you may recall numberless instances of the providential care of that same God…"

Page after page record lives of devotion to God and to prayer and demonstrate how far-reaching lives of faith can be. The influence of those who love God far outlasts their time on earth and touches lives hundreds of years into the future. Not because their life stories are written down but because their prayers are recorded in heaven and their acts of faithfulness are known by God. *Then those who feared the LORD talked with each other, and the LORD listened and heard. A scroll of remembrance was written in his presence concerning those who feared the LORD and honored his name.* (Malachi 3:16)

In His great love,
Laura

O Holy One, lead us in faithful living and give words to our prayers so that generations to come may be blessed. We ask this for the sake of Your kingdom and in Jesus' name. Amen.

But he knows the way that I take; when he has tested me,
I will come forth as gold. My feet have closely followed his steps;
I have kept to his way without turning aside.

—JOB 23:10-11

3 NOVEMBER

Dear Friends,

Since 1986, the U.S. Mint has issued American Eagle proofs—beautiful gold coins struck in various denominations from five to fifty dollars. When my husband and I wanted to commemorate our son's eighteenth birthday in a special way, and we discovered that these coins had first been issued in the very month and year of Peter's birth, we knew we had found just the gift. The coin we bought was presented to us in a velvet-lined box that opens like a book. The coin itself is protected by mylar, but both front and back are visible and the images imprinted in the gold are stunning.

Proof coins are not like the change rattling around in our pockets. They are the same in size, shape and design, but the differences are what matter. Proofs are made of precious metals—Peter's is 91.67% gold—and they differ from other coins in their sharp detail and brilliant, mirror-like surface. They are not produced to pay for a pack of gum or even a diamond ring—they are intended for display. "In the world but not of the world," if you will. Circulated coins are struck a single time but proofs are often struck twice to accentuate the design. They are produced on coining presses adapted just for them with specially polished dies that ensure the greatest clarity of image. Coins are rated based on how worn they are from circulation and proofs get the highest grade— "Perfect Uncirculated."

Peter's coin came to mind today as I listened to a commentary on God's testing of Abraham. "Tested is better translated proved," the speaker said. God does not test us to discover what we believe or what we are going to do. He knows. Rather, with every test He is calling forth a demonstration of our faith. He wants it on display. He is proving us. And we are proving Him. Our every step of obedience validates Christ's message and promises. Every step proves God's power.

How worn are you from circulation? The pain of this world sometimes drives us to our rooms to pray alone, to protect our hearts, to serve in solitude. And in time He gently calls us out again. We are called out as His visual, His Power Point—a display of His power that others can point to. Living out our faith in plain sight makes the Christ life tangible and real to others. We are in His book and we are protected by Him, safe and shining. We are not created to be spent on earthly pleasures but to display the brilliance and purity of His precious substance. We are here to reflect what we are—God's proof of His promises.

With you in Christ,
Laura

Holy Spirit, shine forth from me so blindingly that none can see my stumbling, my scowls. Amen

When you pass through the waters, I will be with you . . .

—ISAIAH 43:2

10 NOVEMBER

Dear Friends,

Very early one morning last winter I went to swim laps at the local community pool. I had the pool to myself at that hour with one exception—in the lane next to me was a young boy, perhaps eight years old, swimming hard. On the pool deck, striding up and down beside him was a woman in a fur coat with a steaming cup of coffee in her leather-gloved hands. She offered frequent and loud correction to the child, who I assume was her son. Lap after lap he swam, and lap after lap she critiqued him.

Throughout my swim I prayed to our Helper, our Teacher, the One continually working with us on our form. "Thank You, God, that You are not a Father who stands apart from my life shouting directions and criticism at me. You are here in the cold water with me. You are holding me up, encouraging me, showing me how it's done. Your voice is kind and close at my ear."

I need not call loudly to You to be heard. You are here. I don't have to know all the strokes. You know them. I don't have to form them perfectly to earn Your approval. You don't require me to perform in a certain manner to make You look good.

Thank You that You love me. I am flailing, failing, not very graceful in the water. But You love me. I am not alone. And that hot, steaming, sweet cup in Your hand is my cup too. Warmth and comfort are mine as Yours.

There is a plan, there is a destination. I am not swimming mindless laps leading nowhere. Thank You for that. Something is being accomplished. Something lasting and good. And You are with me in it. You know the end from the beginning.

Feet touching bottom or carried along by a current, I am not swept away. I am never at the mercy of the water, though I sometimes think I am. You are with me. You are over the waters. You are moving me through.

And may I never be the one striding alongside someone else who is struggling in the water to get it right. May I never be that sure, smug voice from the comfort of the sidelines.

Thank You for the weightlessness of being in the water. The lack of pressure. For the buoyancy of it, and the fun. In the water I pretend to fly. I curl myself up, I twirl. I lie back and rest on the surface of the water, watching the sky, the clouds. I am Yours.

In Isaiah 44 You promise to pour and pour and pour out—water on the thirsty land, streams on the dry ground and, O! Your Spirit on our children! Your blessing on our descendants! They will spring up, You say, like grass in a meadow, like poplar trees by flowing streams.

Flowing streams, still waters, age-old river. Who is this? *He commands even the winds and the water, and they obey him.* (Luke 8:25).

Who is this? You are Father, Teacher, Companion, You cheer us on. Living Water, we praise Your name. Amen.

*Ah, Sovereign LORD, you have made the heavens and the earth by
your great power and outstretched arm. Nothing is too hard for you.*

— JEREMIAH 32:17

17 NOVEMBER

Dear Friends,

I have been drawn to that verse from Jeremiah several times this
week. I keep opening to it, and its wording, its truth, delights my
eye and heart. I need such reminders of the truths of who God is.
Without them the command to pray can begin to feel burdensome.

Do you ever worry that you have not prayed enough about
something? Have you experienced that awful moment: "Oh no!
Today is Thursday and Sally's big interview was last Tuesday and I
forgot to pray!" Do you think that something will not come to pass
because you failed to pray? I have.

And then God gently reminds me of who He is and what prayer
is and where I fit into the equation. If I don't pray for something
His plan is not doomed. Prayer is not me accomplishing something.
Prayer is the means by which the Sovereign Lord graciously allows
me to witness and join in what He is doing. Prayer is God inspired
and God led. We do not aimlessly wander off into prayer, unaccom-
panied and undirected, hoping we end up in the right place. Prayer
is not an Outward Bound experience. Prayer begins with God. It
begins with His desire, His objective, His sovereign plan. *(I know
that no plan of Yours can be thwarted.* Job 42:2). It begins with His
plan and then He calls us to pray.

My prayers are initiated by God, not me. And they are initiated
for His purposes, not mine. He does not need me to pray. Prayer is
not something we are commanded to do for Him. Prayer is something we are invited to do with Him. He has given this gift. He offers this privilege of private conversation with Him. Almighty God

wants to speak with you and with me *"as a man speaks with his friend"*. (Exodus 33:11)

We must never to think of prayer as unending work assigned by a demanding boss. None of us is expected to pray about everything. Each of us has been prepared by experience and temperament to care about and pray over different things. Our prayer concerns are the most personal of assignments by a loving Father.

Our conceptions of prayer can limit us, so we need to expand our vocabulary and think about prayer in new ways using what are, perhaps, new terms. Invitation. Privilege. Fortress. Refuge. Gift. Place.

Prayer is experiencing the presence of God.

Prayer is a place. It is the place where we go to sit with our Father, our Counselor, our friend. It is a resting place. A wrestling place. A workshop and a recovery room.

Prayer is a ceremony. It is the formal acknowledgement and agreement that this matter—whatever it may be—is best handled by His hands, not mine. Title is transferred and my heartaches become His. My concerns. My fears. My problems become His. I retain the joys, even as He claims them as His—the joys we own jointly.

> With you in this prayer place,
> Laura

O Father! Thank You that prayer is not burden but blessing. Thank You for opening up this way for me to lift to You everything that matters to me, large and small. More and more, by prayer, lead me into knowing You and loving You and seeing myself as Yours. Amen

I will rejoice in the LORD, I will be joyful in God my Savior.

— HABBAKUK 3:18

NOVEMBER 24

Dear Friends,

While my friend Meg was on vacation years ago, I was at her apartment each day to feed her cat. On the first day, opening a kitchen
drawer in search of a can opener, I found instead an index card ti-
tled "My Wish List." It was Meg's list of the little things she eventually wanted to get for her new apartment. A peach-scented candle
for the bathroom, a two-cup measuring cup . . . It was easy on her
birthday soon after to surprise Meg with the things she most wanted.
She marveled at each gift before I told her the secret of my inspiration.

The Lord knows our wish lists by heart. We secretly suspect that
committing to live for Him means having to lay aside our list and
take up His for us—a list with nothing fun on it but only lots of
religious activity and good deeds. A list without humor or music or
dessert. A list with nothing frivolous on it or peach-scented. A list
that will require a grim face and loads of self discipline and elbow
grease. A list that calls for sensible shoes.

We mourn in advance all the loved things we suspect we will be
required to give up. If we find such delight in them they must be
selfish and not good for us, not spiritual. Riding our horse. Painting.
Reading, solving a puzzle, playing music, tackling a challenge at
work, having a party, running a marathon, playing Monopoly with
our kids, looking at art. Debating politics. Napping. Rapping.

But growing into our Christ life is gain, not loss. It is the fulfill-
ment of our truest self not the subjugation of it. The God who
promises to give you the desires of your heart is the very God who
created that heart. And as He created it, He was kneading into it
every desire and longing your heart would ever have. It was His

way of steering you right into His plan for you, the plan perfectly suited to your passions and personality, experiences and talents. The Lord God made them all. And He did so for the joy of fulfilling your life, not to deny or frustrate you. His plan for you preceded you. His will for your life preceded your desires and passions and talents. He composed those as the means of drawing you into His plan. The delights of your heart were His invention. Your joy is His intention.

There will be delights that we lay aside along the way but they will be relinquished willingly and by choice because something else has grown up to take their place. The Lord will not have His way at the expense of His children but rather through them—through the passions and inclinations and talents that He himself planted in our hearts for this very purpose.

With you in Christ,
Laura

Lord, forgive my narrow view that sometimes sees life with You as loss to me. For all you are doing in me, through me, thank You. For renewing my mind, for refocusing my eyes, for refining my tastes, thank You. More and more You are mine. More and more I am Yours. Amen.

How great is the love the Father has lavished on us, that we should be called children of God! And that is what we are!

—1 JOHN 3:1

1 DECEMBER

Dear Friends,

My brother Jess called me La all his life. When I was a baby, my parents called me Lolly. I was Laurie in third grade since we had two Lauras in Miss Hassell's class—me and Laura Jo Brown. On my thirteenth birthday, my dad announced to Aunt Peggy and the cousins that I was too old to be addressed any longer as La-La. Nevertheless, nearly forty years later I am still La-La to every one of them.

Today, as I signed Laura on a condolence card to an elderly relative, I realized that aged and grieving as he is, he may not remember me clearly. So I added a phrase that I knew would identify me immediately and eliminate any confusion—"Noel's daughter," I wrote.

Noel's daughter. It was my favorite designation as a child, and I heard it often. Among my mother's relatives I was often identified not by name but by my relation to her, one whom we all loved dearly. I was "Noel's child," "Noel's daughter," "Noel's girl." For those who knew her, lovely things sprang to mind at the mention of my mother's name. "Noel" meant long dark hair. It meant kindness, a gentle spirit, a bit of a southern accent. "Noel" brought to remembrance gorgeous singing and piano music. Marvelous smile, beautiful hands, artistic gifts. Being associated with her elevated me. It enlarged me beyond my own little self. *Noel's daughter* was something more than just *Laura*. As hers, I was something finer, more special, of greater potential.

But I, like you, have a more excellent and lasting designation. I am God's child. The Creator of heaven and earth has become my

Father. *Yet to all who received him, to those who believed in his name, he gave the right to become children of God—children born not of natural descent, nor of human decision or a husband's will, but born of God.* (John 1:12).

We bear His name. We bear His image. And He would send us out into each day as His children—sons and daughters with such a strong family resemblance to their Father that anyone spending time with any of us would feel they have been with Him. He would have us reflect Him in our every choice, response, act of compassion. And the continual prayer conversation is a key part of our upbringing as His. Day after day He is at it—training us to yield self will in favor of allowing Him to lead, to comfort, to correct, to strengthen, to show Himself mighty for us and through us. If we will allow it, He will make Himself visible and known in this world.

"I know your Father," someone might say to me or to you. "He is wonderful. You look something like Him. You remind me of Him." What honor! What victory over our human inclinations. May it be so!

Your sister, and God's girl,

Laura

Our Father in heaven, and right here with us, we are Yours. We are home at last. Thank You for bringing us in. Thank You. In the name of Jesus Christ. Amen.

He has delivered us from such a deadly peril, and he will deliver us.
On him we have set our hope that he will
continue to deliver us, as you help us by your prayers.

— 2 CORINTHIANS 1:10-11

8 DECEMBER

Dear Friends,

In 2004, when the summer Olympics were in Greece, my family and I were there visiting my in-laws and spent several afternoons in the Olympic complex attending various events, particularly water polo games.

Game after game we sat in comfort among thousands of spectators all focused in the same direction—the pool—where fourteen players competed. But my eye was often drawn to another group in the arena. All around the periphery of the pool, stationed every few feet stood men and women in uniform. They were the security detail. And the most noteworthy thing about this group was their position. While we all faced the pool, while all our eyes were on the game, their backs were to the pool at all times. In fact, their eyes were on us! We watched the game and they watched us. Their job was to protect the players from any interference or interruption.

Here we were, all in the arena together, hearing the same whistles of the refs, the same shouts of the players, the groans or cheers of the spectators. But all that was just background noise for the security team. They were at work. They missed all the amazing shots, the close calls, the great victories. They missed a lot. But they were engaged in something necessary and important. They were doing their job.

What a wonderful picture of what we do at prayer. An important part of praying for our children, our loved ones, our world, involves anticipating some of the dangers they may face and deflecting them by entrusting them to God. Taking up such a job involves a cost. At times it can feel like loss because the work of prayer will sometimes require that we miss the game, that we work while others play. It asks us to turn our backs to the fun, to relegate earthly considerations to the background while we lift our sights and turn our attention and our energy elsewhere. So this is not a service taken up lightly, nor is it faithfully maintained by very many. But it is most honorable work. It is a position of privilege and of incalculable value. It allows our loved ones to play on in safety.

Our prayers release the power of God Himself. And like security people deliberately stationed in plain sight, the sight of us at prayer, our willingness to standing guard in that way, may itself discourage some evil we know not of.

The members of that Olympic security team were positioned side by side. And we who pray are positioned in exactly the same way. None of us ever prays alone. Remember that He who calls us to it also joins us in it. (Romans 8:34).

> Side by side by side with you
> (and You),
> Laura

Almighty God, may You be honored and known and praised—You who guard our hearts. You, ever standing with us and in us, thank You. In Jesus' name. Amen.

Now to Him who is able to do immeasurably more than all
we ask or imagine, according to his power at work within us,
to him be glory in the church and in Christ Jesus throughout
all generations, for ever and ever! Amen.

—EPHESIANS 3:20-21

5 JANUARY

Dear Friends,

Sometimes a joyful jolt strikes me, a needed reminder. When feeling lonely or faced with a challenge or celebrating a victory, a
thought comes that changes everything. I remember the great truth
that makes all the difference in the world, the truth that, incredibly,
I sometimes forget: I am not alone in this. God is with me. This
burden, this battle, this joy, is not mine alone but shared. It is His,
too.

Jesus Christ lives in me by His Spirit. And it is a holy Spirit. He
is present in me in His full power at all times. Years ago, when I
accepted His forgiveness, when I thanked Christ for the sacrifice
He had made on my behalf, He became my Savior. He joined my
life to His on that day and made His home in me. He became Lord
of my life.

And the government shall be upon His shoulders. The governing
of my life. In His holiness and love He offers to govern each of my
days, each of my challenges, all of my efforts and actions and reactions, if I will allow it. We are not limited to our own abilities or
offerings. We have far more to draw from, to rely upon, to access
than we sometimes remember we have. We are far richer than the
sum of our earthly resources or the accumulated strength or wisdom of our human counselors, coaches or comforters. The Spirit of
God lives in us. The Spirit of Jesus Christ. In fact, it is His very presence within that defines a person as Christian.

As this new year begins, we resolve to do more of this or less of that. We commit to start doing X and stop doing Y or Z. And yet consider this: the Holy Spirit of God has made some resolutions of His own for the upcoming year in your life. And His resolutions will be kept all year long. What the Holy Spirit wants to do in you and through you will be more lasting, more important and better in every way than whatever you have resolved to do in your own strength.

Do you want to know what He has planned, what He has ordained for you this year? Will you work with Him or against Him in bringing about His best for your life? The deciding factor will be prayer. Prayer, His great gift to us and our great gift to Him. Prayer, that time we take to sit companionably with Him who shares our heart space, our body, our life. Prayer, the appointed place and the means by which we yield to Him our thoughts, our loved ones, our planned course.

In this new year may we step out in His power. May we allow Him His way, His will. The only thing that can prevent it is our refusal to yield to His promptings. Our reluctance to relinquish rule. Our hesitancy to trust Him who countless times has proven Himself worthy of our trust. May this new year of ours be His!

Laura

Almighty God, as this year begins we rest safely in Your hand. And when this year comes to a close we will still be safely there. In every day in between may we look to You in trust and love and obedience for the sake of Your honor and Your good and loving will. Amen.

Look to the LORD and his strength; seek his face always.

—PSALM 105:4

12 JANUARY

Dear Friends,

I spent a restless night last week, tired and angrily tossing in bed, cataloging someone's failings against me. I lay there making a list and checking it twice, thrice, endlessly. They were not where they should be. They were not doing what they should be doing. How often had this happened before? How often had their failings cost me? How could they be so selfish?

In the midst of this, a phrase popped into my mind—*"You follow me"*—and I knew just what God was saying to me by it. At the end of John 21, as Jesus is giving some personal instruction to Peter, Peter turns and sees John and asks, *"Lord, what about this man?"* And Jesus says, *"…what is that to you? You follow me."*

What others do or fail to do is not my business. My focus is to be on Him and whatever He is asking me to do. I woke the next morning to an email that made me smile. It was from a friend offering cheer and it was from God offering further correction. It quoted Psalm 63:6-8. *I lie awake thinking of you, meditating on you through the night. I think how much you have helped me; I sing for joy in the shadow of your protecting wings. I follow close behind you; your strong right hand holds me securely.*

When I am lying awake in my bed, I am to be meditating on God, thinking about how much He has helped me, not enumerating all the ways others have not. And, (here it was again) I am to be following Him. And following closely, so closely that He can reach out and take hold of me.

To follow Him my eyes need to be on Him and not on others. In John 21:19-20, in that conversation between Jesus and Peter, the two words that come after "Follow me" are the ones to note. *Then he said to him, "Follow me!" Peter turned...* Jesus said "follow me" and Peter turned away to look at John. When we turn from Him, we get off track. All week I turned to watch others, to consider them and their choices. But day and night He kept calling to me, urging me to refocus on Him and what He is asking me to do.

"Follow Me" were perhaps Christ's final words of personal instruction to Peter, and I notice that according to Matthew (4:19) and Mark (1:17) they also were the first words He had spoken to him years before when He first called Peter as a disciple. His message to Peter, to you, to me, is consistent from first to last: Follow Me. Keep your eyes, your focus, on Me.

It is not some anonymous back or pair of shoulders we are asked to follow. His loving face is turned toward us. To follow speaks of attitude as well as action. A follower is one in the service of another. My favorite definition of a follower is this: "a machine part that receives motion from another part." We are to receive our motion from Him. Not to initiate any of our own apart from His leading.

To follow Christ is not to imitate Him. It is not me acting like Him. It is Him acting through me. It is me yielding, surrendering, allowing Him to inhabit me and entirely control my movements, direction, pace and purpose. We are asked not to hand over all to some faceless dictator, but to be relieved of all by the Father of compassion, our counselor, refiner and King.

> Your fellow failing,
> forgiven follower,
> Laura

Keep calling me back, Father. Do not allow me to stray from You and Your best for me. Amen.

Prepare the way of the Lord, make straight paths for him.

— MATTHEW 3:3

19 JANUARY

Dear Friends,

As I made my way along the walking trail behind our house on Saturday afternoon, I noted with annoyance a cigarette butt on the path, and then another. A step or two later there was another and farther along, a plastic bag from a fast food place. I picked up the bag and went back to collect the trash I'd seen. After that, my walk slowed as I kept my eyes to the ground. Instead of admiring trees and sky, I was picking up a bit of wrapper every few steps or some broken glass. I bent down for more cigarettes, plastic, packaging. Everything I picked up was small, barely noticeable, and yet my bag filled little by little. The cigarette butts alone numbered close to sixty before I got home. It was not the walk I'd envisioned but it was a good one, and necessary. And anyone who comes along afterward will benefit.

Earlier that day I had spent some prayer time admitting a number of small failings, annoyances, wrong choices. Looking back in my prayer journal for that morning I am surprised to see how many things I enumerated and handed over to Him. I don't remember it being so many, but I'm grateful to see that it was, that my confession was so wide-ranging.

When challenged by circumstances and demands, as I have been lately, times of prayer are welcome and needed oases of peace and His strengthening. But He had something different in mind for this Saturday prayer time of mine, something I hadn't planned. He had taken a walk through my thoughts and heart, back through my week, and unexpectedly set me to work then bending down to take up a host of things that didn't belong on the pathway between us. He called me to honest confession about various small faults and resentments that didn't look like much individually, but every one of which was out of place in a heart intent upon serving Him and His purposes in this world. And once I handed them over, He carried all of it away. I don't know where He tosses them but He promises that He does, and I need never see them again. And as always, anyone who came along afterward, anyone I encountered through the rest of that Saturday, benefited from my time with Him.

If I had cherished sin in my heart, the Lord would not have listened, but God has surely listened and heard my voice in prayer. (Psalm 66:18-19) Repentance and confession are vital to keeping the prayer channel open and clean. They prepare the way for Him. Christ can only pour into this world if we will be diligent about unburdening ourselves of anything that would impede His unhindered flow through us. My mother-in-law tells me that in the Greek village of her youth, girls went out to cut brooms from the aromatic brush and chaparral on the hillsides. For the clean sweep that clears and straightens His way, confession is our sweet-smelling broom.

in His love,
Laura

Almighty God, when we don't notice the litter at our feet, at Your feet, You notice. Thank You for calling us to confess all that we might be content to overlook. You don't make excuses for us or justify it when we sin. Thank You for the relief of the truth. And for Your promise to forgive anything that we will confess. Amen.

I wait for the Lord, my soul waits, and in his word I put my hope.

— PSALM 130:5

26 JANUARY

Dear Friends,

Just before Christmas I asked my Aunt Jane for a present. "I have a silver bracelet with charms on it from a lot of loved ones who are important to me and I'd like to have you represented on my bracelet. Would you pick out a charm for me?"

Jane phoned a day or two later. "I have your charms. I got eight of them!"

Eight! That wasn't what I wanted at all, not what I'd asked for. She must have misunderstood. I responded with annoyance, without gratitude or grace.

When I went to Jane's house, there on her dining table were eight little packets. Each one had a name on top and a note handwritten by Jane. I saw my mother's name on one. "Nöel loved all kinds of birds, especially the dove for peace. May she rest in peace. With love for your bracelet." A little bird from my mother. There was my brother Nick's name. The cluster of red hearts stood for the love of his family, said Jane. My aunt Rowena, whose wisdom and counsel I dearly miss, is represented by a little owl. A dangling charm that spoke to Jane of the unhindered movement of the Holy Spirit had my late brother Jess's name on it. A shamrock, hearts, a dolphin, birds, flowers. The notes were funny and the choices dear. "Since I eat a can of sardines daily, it was easy for me to pick this lovely fish for your charm bracelet. Love, Auntie Jane." What a gift of abundance, of sensitivity, of love. Jane knew better than I what gifts my heart most wanted.

When their brother Lazarus was ill, Mary and Martha must surely have felt that Jesus had misunderstood their request. They had sent word to Him, *"Lord, the one you love is sick."* (John 11:3)

And His unlikely response is recorded in verse 6. When He heard that Lazarus was sick, He stayed where He was two more days. Jesus stayed where He was and Lazarus died. This could not have been what the sisters expected. But God was preparing something greater than what they sought.

And His motive in allowing the heartache is stated. *Now Jesus loved Martha and her sister and Lazarus. So, when he heard that Lazarus was ill, he stayed two days longer in the place where he was.* (John 11:5-6 ESV). Jesus loved them and so He allowed the loss. Because His intention and plan were joyful reunion, deeper faith and glory to God. The sisters did not grieve without purpose. Neither did they grieve alone. Verse 35 tells us that Jesus wept with them.

What would have happened if Mary or Martha had taken herself off to her room, as I might have done. What if, in their distress or disappointment with Jesus, they had decided to keep their distance from Him for a while. A bit of the silent treatment, perhaps. Imagine what they would have missed—the gift, the miracle, the sight of their beloved brother stepping out of his tomb and into daylight and into their arms.

Has something come into your life that is not what you asked for? Something that makes you think that God misheard your prayer? That He misunderstands your desire or need? He understands better than you realize. Better, even, than you do. Only hang on. He is working on a grand scale. Keep talking to Him, patiently listening, watching. Trust Him who loves you so dearly.

Laura

Lord, when I want to turn away in pain or sullenness, when I am failing to trust, keep me close! Don't allow me to miss a bit of Your blessing and bounty. For Your glory, Amen.

Our help is in the name of the Lord, the Maker of heaven and earth.

— PSALM 124:8

2 FEBRUARY

Dear Friends,

When my friend Meg was near death, I didn't know how to pray. Certainly I prayed for her healing, but other things came to mind that I thought I should be praying for her family in case she did not recover. Did my anticipating her death suggest a lack of faith in God's ability to heal? I worried about that. Was I indulging in dangerous negative thinking? Could I be jinxing His plans for her recovery? Was I being disloyal as a friend to pray anything beyond, "Please heal her"?

My thoughts and emotions were tangled. "Tell me how to pray for her," I asked God as I drove to a meeting at church. "I don't know what to say!" At that instant I slowed for a red light and the car alongside me turned and pulled away. Its license plate said: "Pslm 51". I had just enough time before the light changed to open the Bible on the seat beside me and read the first few words of Psalm 51, *Have mercy on me, O God, according to your unfailing love; according to your great compassion . . . "*

Here was just the reminder I needed of Who God is. Merciful. Compassionate. Unfailingly loving. I was reminded that it is He who controls what happens, not me or my thoughts or words. In that single verse He supplied just the prayer I (and Meg) needed, "Have mercy on Meg, Father, whatever Your plan for her may be," I prayed. "According to Your unfailing love. According to your great compassion."

When our eyes drop from Him and His power, and settle instead on ourselves, we can get mixed up about our part in life and in prayer. We fear that our prayers might limit Him—one wrong, misplaced or forgotten word and all is lost. Or conversely we credit ourselves with the ability to bypass Him completely and determine the outcome ourselves. I had an email this week asking me to send my positive thoughts and energy to a woman who is ill. Such a request reflects the very human desire to believe that we can control what happens. It suggests that our thoughts have a power equal to God's. To claim to have such a power, indeed to claim any of the attributes of deity, is the very definition of blasphemy.

God alone has the power to heal, to make whole, to give life. We do not pray to control circumstances or to control God, but seeking His best. We go to Him in prayer exactly because we recognize that the power to determine outcomes is His alone. Prayer, then, is the opposite of trusting in ourselves or our positive thinking. We turn to Him in humility, well aware of our powerlessness, our need and inadequacy. And we turn to Him in joy and relief with trust and confidence in His plan, His might, His mercy.

praying with you,
Laura

Almighty God, all power is Yours, not mine. You control things and I don't. Thank You for the great unchanging truth of Your sovereignty. Amen.

The Lord is righteous in all his ways and loving toward all
he has made . . . My mouth will speak in praise of the Lord.
Let every creature praise his holy name for ever and ever.

9 FEBRUARY

—PSALM 145:17, 21

Dear Friends,

Thirteen years ago we picked out two kittens at the shelter. They were brothers born on Halloween, so our son named them Boo and Shadow. There was a few days' wait for paperwork and shots before we could bring them home, but in the meantime we visited. On one visit we found Boo alone in their cage, which was worrisome. But, turning, we saw Shadow. Another visitor was walking around with him in her arms, petting him and laughing as he licked her arm. The sight of it bothered me—this was our kitty! We had not yet brought him into our family but I felt jealous and protective.

The Bible says God feels the same way about us. Even before He brings us into His family He watches over us protectively, jealously. He wants us for His own and looks eagerly toward that day when we will accept His forgiveness and Lordship and enter into our lives as His.

Our cats have always been housecats because there are coyotes in the area. But one evening Shadow got out, which we didn't notice for hours. It was near midnight when we began to search the house and yard and then got in the car to drive slowly through the neighborhood. We found him at the bottom of our street. He wasn't far from home, sitting in the road meowing, lost, shaking with cold. I called his name as I approached and talked to him as I scooped him up. I held him on my lap in the warm car as my husband drove us home.

The One who loves us comes after us when we get lost, when we have wandered away from His side and can't remember the way back. When we are sitting in an unfamiliar place seemingly far from comfort, from trusting, from responding His way to the challenges that inevitably come, He will draw us back with neither condemnation nor hesitation. I wrote to a friend this week, "I know I have gotten off track spiritually in recent weeks and I am homesick for the feel of His hand on my head." Recognizing the problem as a spiritual one, and acknowledging my part in it restored to me that sense of His nearness. He, of course, had not moved. Home for the child of God is obedience to the will of God.

Years ago, when Shadow broke his leg, he withdrew in his pain and hid himself in the linen closet. But I drew him out and my son and I took him for the surgery he needed, grieving over his pain as we went. Well-cared for and well-loved, he healed beautifully.

God carries us when we can't walk, when we want to hide, when we try to tend to our pain in private. He takes us where He knows we need to go. We are not consigned to a dark, lonely place to lick our wounds in solitude. He hurts with us and is our very present help as the breaks are set, as the sore places heal. His hand is on us. We are not alone.

Last Friday and Saturday nights I lay on the floor alongside aging, ailing Shadow. I held him, I talked to him. I even read him some psalms, starting with the one (148) that tells every created thing to praise God—the angels and stars, the water and wind, mountains and all hills, fruit trees and beasts and flying birds. "That means you, Shadow," I told him "and me, too."

We are to praise Him. Even when it's hard. Even when we hurt. Even on a day like last Sunday when Shadow died, my husband's hand and mine on his head, our words of love in his ear.

Laura

We praise You, God of all creation. We praise You, Creator of every two- and four-legged creature that You give us to care for and by whom You comfort us and teach us to love. Amen.

. . . when the people willingly offer themselves—praise the LORD!

—JUDGES 5:2

16 FEBRUARY

Dear Friends,

God has been asking me to do something difficult. I talked to Him about it this morning.

"Will You do it for me, Lord? I can't do it."

"Can't or won't?"

"What?"

"Are you unable to do it or unwilling? Is your heart willing to do it?"

(No, my heart is not willing to do it. In fact, to tell you the truth I resent the assignment. And I have been refusing to do it. I've been asking Him to do it because I don't want to.)

"Will You do it?" I ask God.

"Will you do it?" God asks me.

He will not do for me what I refuse to do for Him. My willingness (or lack thereof) became the focus of our prayer time today. He showed me how hard my heart has been about this matter. As long as I refuse to yield I am hindering what He wants to do in me and through me. And I want to be a stepping stone for Him, not an impediment. I want to be working with Him not against Him.

I tried another tack. "I wouldn't mind doing this job, Lord, if only I had been asked first. It feels like it was thrust upon me. I'd just like to feel I have a choice."

"You were given a choice," He said to me. "You were asked, and you said yes."

"When?"

"October 1988. When you agreed to my Lordship over your life.

"Oh. Yes."

'My will' means the way I want things to go. And God is asking me to yield that to Him in favor of the way He wants things to go. The only thing you or I can give to God that He does not already control is our will. That is all we can decide to give to Him. Everything else is His already.

"If you are willing, you can make me clean," the leper said to Christ. (Mark 1:40).

If you are willing, I can make you Mine, Christ says to me and to you. If you are willing I can dwell in you with power and I can move in this world using you as my instrument. If you are willing, I can even make you willing. *I will give you a new heart and put a new spirit in you; I will remove from you your heart of stone and give you a heart of flesh.* (Ezekiel 36:26).

Laura

Lord God, I pray "Thy will be done," but usually I only want Your will to be done if it's not going to cost me. Overrule me and my preferences and even my prayers when they are opposed to Your will. And in any area where I am battling You for control, may the victory be Yours, and quickly. Amen.

Give thanks to the LORD Almighty,
for the LORD is good; his love endures forever.

— JEREMIAH 33:11

23 FEBRUARY

Dear Friends,

Virtually every day my mother-in-law, Dimitra, uses one or more of her set of six graduated mixing bowls. This was the perfect gift for her and is the most useful and used item in her kitchen. When she got them for Christmas several years ago, she raved for weeks afterward about what an ideal gift my friend Pat had given her. Except that Pat hadn't chosen and bought the set—I had. But when Pat was over one day and sought my advice for a gift that would perfectly suit Dimitra, I suggested she give her the bowls.

Every December Dimitra gets out the little tabletop brass Christmas tree she delights in. As she decorates it and chooses the perfect spot for each of the colored balls, she sings the praises of Amy, the houseguest who left the tree as a thank-you gift after a long-ago visit. But Amy didn't choose or purchase the tree or the decorations. I had seen and bought them knowing they were just the thing for Dimitra. Later, when Amy asked for help in finding a house gift Dimitra was sure to love, I gave her the tree and ornaments.

Dimitra is as happy with her gifts as I knew she would be. And for years I have enjoyed watching her enjoy them. But I do feel an occasional sting that I am not the one to be acknowledged or thanked for those just-right selections.

How often this happens to God! All of us can look back and name one instance after another of the most remarkable perfect timing. Yet over and over we fail to give God the credit. We forget Him as the Author of events, as the Power at work all around us, as the Giver of every good gift, as the source of all that we have and all that we need. When things work out well, we credit coincidence, chance, karma, synchronicity, luck, or the alignment of the stars. When friends appear with just the word we need, we marvel at their intuition, sensitivity, sixth sense. We praise the gene pool that gave our child a pleasant physical feature or personality. We take pride in and credit for our own talents and natural gifts, forgetting our Creator.

We may simply resolve to live a more thankful life. We may count our blessings. But even that can be little more than an exercise in list making with no thought given to God and no word to Him. Every gift, every instance of things falling beautifully into place should be a thrilling reminder and confirmation of His presence, His power, and His purposeful movement in this world. Gratitude follows naturally, and expressing our thanks then becomes a central part of our prayer conversation, as it should be. When we remember to remember our God, when our thoughts are full of Him, our eyes more and more will be open to His authorship and goodness. And our hearts will offer Him the thanks and praise that are His due.

Laura

All honor and glory are rightly Yours, Father. May Your days, Your ears, be filled with our thanks. Amen.

I will never leave you nor forsake you.

—JOSHUA 1:5

30 MARCH

Dear Friends,

I visited MIT recently, a university notorious for its academic intensity and high pressure. A vending machine I passed offered all the expected snacks along with a most incongruous one—animal crackers. The sight of it in that particular setting was both funny to me and touching. In times of challenge, in need of comfort, we often reach for emblems of a former, easier time.

When I reach into my purse for keys or phone, my hand inevitably brushes against a linen handkerchief of my father's that sits in the bottom of my bag. The fabric is softened with age and no longer bright white but still pressed into the little four-inch square that my father used to slip into his hip pocket each morning. From the looks of it he might have carried this one with him over several years. I have carried it with me for twenty more. In my heart and memory, this little patch represents comfort to me. Throughout my childhood it dealt admirably with whatever tears, milk mustache, scratched finger, or running mascara that needed attending to. In the years since he died I have clutched it during speaking engagements and patted it in my pocket during medical procedures. I don't regard it as a good luck charm, it is simply familiar and reassuring, a reminder of another time and of my father's seeming ability to take care of whatever came up.

Even as that handkerchief represents to me something more, so do our earthly fathers stand for something greater. Our fathers typify—sometimes poorly, sometimes well—what God is to us, Father to child. In 1906 S.D. Gordon wrote, "'Father' stands for strength, loving strength. A father plans, and provides for, and protects his loved ones...God is a father, only He is so much finer a father than the finest father you ever knew of... And His will for your life down here these days is a father's will for the one most dearly loved."

You are the one most dearly loved. So am I. And our sure knowledge of His presence with us and His love for us and His power available to us will be the greatest comfort we can carry with us through life. He is our very present help. And prayer is the means by which we call Him into every circumstance—the mundane, the joyful, the overwhelming. It is immensely significant that when Jesus taught the disciples to pray He began with the words, "Our Father." What could more clearly or succinctly have conveyed all that is ours as His? At any and every moment we have it within our power to step out of this noisy, demanding world to meet with our Father, the One who loves us as no other.

What emblem will our children carry with them into adulthood? Years from now, during a difficult time, what will they reach for when they seek the relief and comfort of an earlier time? May it be the hand of their Father. And may that reach for Him be fondly familiar from long experience. May they turn, with full confidence, to Him. Let us pray our children will pray.

Laura

Our Father, thank You that You are with us always. In every direction are evidences of Your Father love. We are safe as Yours. Keep us close. Keep us close. Amen.

. . . let the hearts of those who seek the LORD rejoice!

—PSALM 105:3

6 APRIL

Dear Friends,

Psalm 105 begins beautifully. *Oh, give thanks to the LORD; call upon his name; make known his deeds among the peoples! Sing to him, sing praise to him; tell of all his wonderful works!* What a great recipe for prayer—thank Him, call upon Him, sing to Him, praise Him. And then go out and tell all the wonderful things He has done for you. The psalmist goes on to do just that, to make known His deeds. What follows is a remarkable record of God's faithfulness and of His movement in this world on behalf of His people. Our God is living and active, and active in a myriad of ways. Those of us who turn to Him have every reason for thanksgiving, for peace of mind, for joy. Remember Who it is you are calling to and relying upon to answer your need. All power is His. In this psalm alone:

He pronounces
He allows
He chooses
He makes fruitful
He judges
He turns hearts
He remembers
He destroys
He confirms
He proves true
He rebukes
He shatters trees
He calls down famine
He speaks

He sends a man
He guards
He sends darkness
He gives
He authors miraculous signs
He turns waters to blood
He turns rain to hail
He strikes down vines
He brings out Israel, laden with silver and gold
He spreads out a cloud as a covering
He sends fire to give them light at night
He brings them quail
He satisfies them with the bread of heaven
He opens a rock and water gushes out
He remembers his holy promise
He brings out his people with rejoicing, his chosen ones
     with shouts of joy.

Rejoice!
Laura

Almighty God, may every demonstration of Your power, Your sovereignty and Your benevolence lift our thoughts to You. May they cause us to praise You and to entrust more and more of our lives and our loved ones into Your keeping. You alone are worthy of all praise and trust. Amen.

Father, I thank you that you have heard me.

— JOHN 11:41

13 APRIL

Dear Friends,

I remember what a help it was to me to be taught the ACTS acronym as a guide for my praying. Years later it remains an easy way when I pray to remember to include Adoration (or praise), Confession, Thanks and Supplication (or asking for whatever is needed). But there is more to prayer than is suggested by any recipe or framework or grid we may use as a helpful guideline. I have been thinking lately about an aspect of prayer that is neither thanking nor praising. It is not asking for anything or apologizing. It's just talking to God without necessarily seeking help or an answer. It's conversational and easy.

When I pray this way, it doesn't sound like prayer in the conventional sense. I tell God what I've been thinking about. In His hearing I muse over things. I reminisce. Occasionally it occurs to me that I am telling God something He already knows. But of course anything we say to God is something He already knows. We pray not to inform Him but to include Him.

I didn't notice this part of my prayer conversation until I began to write out my prayers as I pray. Writing them out was recommended to me as a way to keep focused during prayer time, which it accomplishes very well. But writing my prayers also intensifies the sense of communicating one-on-one with the Father. And it leaves me with an invaluable record of whom I have prayed for and what I have prayed and when I brought a particular concern to God. Sometimes writing out my prayers gives me a surprise. I believe it was Joan Didion who said, "I write to find out what I'm thinking." I pray to find out what I'm thinking. And I pray to find out what God is thinking. In conversation with Him I find out who I really am—I say to Him those things I can say to no one else.

When we have something to confess, God is the One we must go to. When we want to praise Him, to Him we go. When we want to thank Him for His gifts and blessings, we turn to Him. When we need something, we naturally ask the One who can do all things. But we can go anywhere for conversation, we can share our thoughts and impressions and disappointments and annoyances with any number of loved ones. So when we choose Him, when we come to Him just to talk, I think it must particularly delight Him. It is a gift we have given. I feel that way whenever my son calls seeking nothing, just to talk. I was friends for years with Clara, but I can tell you exactly when I believed for the first time how much I meant to her. It was when she called me in the middle of one night needing to talk. She needed a listener and could have called any number of people, but she called me. What an honor.

In the same way, we can honor Him. Choosing Him to talk things over with is a way to let Him know what He means to us.

Healed, held, heard,
Chatty Cathy

When You want to share Your life with us, may we listen to You as willingly as You listen to us. May we be as eager to catch every word. We pray as Yours, in Jesus' name. Amen.

On the last and greatest day of the Feast, Jesus stood and said
in a loud voice, "If anyone is thirsty, let him come to me and drink.

— JOHN 7:37

20 APRIL

Dear Friends,

Hungry? In Spanish we say "tengo hambre," "I have hunger." It is something we have temporarily. In English we say "I am hungry." The hunger defines us.

Do your hungers define you? Mine did for many years. There is a great difference, though, between listing some truths about yourself and defining yourself by them.

What is your primary self definition? Parent? Athlete? Professional? Neglected? Widowed? Attorney? Cancer Patient? Spouse? Orphan? Wealthy? Ignored?

John was one of the disciples who spent the most time with Jesus. And four times in the Gospel of John he identifies himself not by name, but as "the disciple whom Jesus loved". Not only did he know Jesus loved him, he defined himself by that fact. That is what time in God's presence did for him. That is what time in God's presence can do for us. That is the importance and promise of our daily time with Him.

Difficulties will come anyway. They are part of life in this world. But if He loves us, and He does, if He is holy and merciful, and He is, if He allows hard things to happen, and He does, we have to take it on faith that there is something more going on or being worked out than our limited earthly perspective can understand. There will come a time when we will see it in full. In the meantime we have to trust Him. That is the very definition of faith—to trust Him in it now, before it's all spelled out for us someday. And Faith invites us to define ourselves by our relation to Him, not by those things that happen to us.

I have a black belt in self pity. I am an ace. And as I have thought lately about the difference between self pity and sadness it seems to me that the difference is one of attitude. Self pity has arrogance at its core. Self pity says, "I don't deserve this. This should not have happened. This is not acceptable to me." An affronted tone says to God, "How dare you!"

Instead, as we yield ourselves to His love, as we recognize and acknowledge His authority over us, we are enabled to lower our heads humbly and to say to God, "As You wish," as Westley did to Buttercup, in "The Princess Bride". Over and over and all our lives. Sometimes we can sing it wholeheartedly and other times we have to force the words out of an angry mouth. But our lives as His should be marked increasingly with acceptance of His rule. With belief in His sovereignty. With unfailing trust in His unfailing love.

John 15:16 leapt off the page at me one day, *You did not choose me but I chose you* . . . He chose me. I have been chosen. I am home. I can stop my striving now. That day I wrote this as I prayed: "May this be the day peace comes. May this be the day I lay down the self identity 'I am hungry' and take up the identity 'I am chosen.' I am God's. I am the Father's and the Father is mine.

Laura

Lord God, You say in Isaiah that our strength is in quietness and trust. As Yours, may we know ourselves strong. As Yours, may we know ourselves. We pray in Jesus' name. Amen.

All the days ordained for me were written
in your book before one of them came to be.

—PSALM 139:16

27 APRIL

Dear Friends,

In every day of my existence, in every day of your existence, all the way back to the start, in every circumstance of our lives, God has been present in His full power and working with a purpose, accomplishing His holy, loving will. Our current circumstances are not random, and the events of our pasts were not random. He reigns.

I used to think that God didn't concern Himself with my life until the day He brought me to spiritual life and I accepted His forgiveness. I imagined that on that day that He came into my life and looked around, thoughtfully considering options, and then took up some of the mess and a few of the scraps of my past and began to piece together something passable. Like trying to make a meal out of dried-out, questionable leftovers. I pictured Him gamely improvising some sort of future for me out of my mishandled opportunities and past heartaches.

But that's not the way it was. Not for any of us. God does not sweep in after the fact to consider your past and mine. He was there in it. He was there before it. He was ruling over it and through it. The day God made you alive in Christ was not the day He became active in your life. He already was. That was not the day He became sovereign over all the details of your life. He already was. That was not the day He began to reign in your life with full power. He has reigned from the start. *And he shall reign forever and ever.*

The great hope we have in the sovereign, loving God is not only a present hope, not only a hope for the future, but it is a hope that extends backward into our past as well. Before you knew Him, He knew you. Before you were living for Him, He was living for you.

Can you look back and see the Lord at work in your childhood or early life? He was there. He is present now and He was present then. Can you recognize some of the people and circumstances He used to draw you to Him? Do you look back and see pain and chaos? He was there. Do you see carefree days and security? He was there. Whatever you see when you look back, it does not represent a failure of God's love for you.

His love for us has never failed. He was sovereign over every circumstance and relationship and loss that formed you and me. And as we come to know this truth about Him and to accept it, we will begin to see the events of our lives in a very different light. It will change the way we look at our past. And it will change the way we talk about it. Even the tone of voice we use when we talk about it will be different. And we may less readily assign blame to the people involved. We will look past them to Him who loves us. We will look through the tangle of earthly circumstances to Him who is trustworthy, to Him who rules in all things, at all times.

His with you,
Laura

All praise to You, Almighty God, who was and is and is to come. All honor is Yours. Amen.

*. . . you were washed, you were sanctified, you were justified in
the name of the Lord Jesus Christ and by the Spirit of our God*

— 1 CORINTHIANS 6:11

4 MAY

Dear Friends,

I took a bath last week. This is greater news than it may appear to
be—it was my first bath in almost three months. With an open sur-
gical wound on my back I had been limited to showers. They have
kept me as clean as a whistle, and I like the efficiency of a quick
shower, but I did miss those late-night hot soaks. I like to review my
day in the tub and plan for tomorrow, and from a bath I head to bed
relaxed and quieted and ready for sleep. I will always remember the
greatest bath of my life. Never have I eased my sore body into hot
water with greater joy or appreciation. An hour earlier I had given
birth to my son, my ten-pound son. No bath has ever been more
perfect reward, rest, place of rejoicing.

As I jumped in and out of the shower this morning in under
four minutes, it reminded me of the quick prayers I pray throughout the day. As I go about my daily business I repeatedly jump into
God's presence and get the cleansing or answers or direction I need.
There's always time for that. And those short prayers along the way
give me quick spritzes of Him that allow me to keep spreading the
aroma of Christ.

And then there is another kind of prayer. The portion of the day
when we choose to slow down to be alone with Him is like slipping
into a spiritual bathtub. Long, warm, prayerful soaks in His presence are very different in character from our on-the-run praying,
and they serve us differently. In more focused prayer time we are
able to take in what He would say to us of who He is, of who we are,
of how we are doing as parents, as spouses, as His. He will review
with us what is happening in our lives and will prepare us for what

is to come. He will entrust to us important truths and confidences only when He knows He has our undivided attention. In every relationship the most personal words of love are spoken in one-on-one time, and it is no different in our lives with Him. Hearts are shared and knit together in quiet, extended conversations.

Time apart with God is increasingly necessary as the pace of our world speeds up and its volume increases. We need quiet to gather our thoughts. We need calm to revisit and digest the day's events and experiences. Soaking ourselves in His presence does so much more than cleanse us spiritually. It softens the parts of us that have become calloused and hard. Time with Him refreshes what has become dry and brittle. It relaxes tense muscles.

Make time each day for focused, unhurried conversation with Him. As long as we refuse to stop, feel, think or listen, we are in danger of racing through shallow lives, spiritually dull and unavailable to God. My husband, a flash-flood researcher, reminds me that the water that replenishes the earth and refills underground reservoirs is not runoff but the slower-moving water that soaks in. And new growth that springs out of soaked soil can feed and nourish and revive a multitude.

> with pruney fingers and toes,
> Laura

Our Father, thank You for the warm, clean, soothing, softening, comfort of life as Yours. Amen.

. . . the LORD turns my darkness into light.

— 2 SAMUEL 22:29

11 MAY

Dear Friends,

I spent a glad month at summer camp when I was twelve. I remember with particular fondness the three nights each week that we spent sitting around a fire singing, swatting at mosquitoes, putting on skits, laughing and listening to staff talks. On campfire nights all ninety of us, a noisy happy group, would leave our cabins after supper and head across the field to the fire ring. After we had settled into our seats we would look around to see who was missing. Someone always was. Because at some point in the evening a camper would have been tapped on the shoulder and pulled out of the crowd. She would have missed the relaxed walk to the fire ring with the rest of us. She would have missed the laughter and chatter and the choosing of seats. Instead, she would have been taken behind Cabin #1 and congratulated. She had been chosen by the staff as torchbearer, the camp's highest honor. And after receiving instructions, a torch was placed in her hand and she was sent out on a run by herself from down near the lake, up past the cabins and across the field to the place where the rest of us waited.

We would be watching for the flame, excited, expectant. Long before we could identify the runner, the flame would be visible in the dark and we marked its progress. It grew larger and brighter as it drew closer. And when the runner finally entered our circle—all of us craning our necks to see who it was—she had the privilege of lighting our campfire.

Three friends all in different life circumstances and seasons have mentioned the feeling recently of having been set aside, cut off from friends, removed from the action, missing the fun, required to be home or even in bed more than they would choose to be. And I am reminded of that runner. The girl who was pulled out of our midst, who missed some of what we got to do. The one who had to make her way without her friends around her.

Alone, it might not have felt like an honor. It might even have been frightening to be asked to run alone across a Texas field in darkness, in silence, in summer, with any number of creatures flying low or slithering or tunneling in the dark. She had been asked to do something not asked of everyone. She arrived winded. But she also arrived exhilarated. And her run in the dark inspired and served the whole group because when she came she brought light with her and its warmth. And its power set things crackling and popping for all of us.

Is God is asking you to be alone or silent or in the dark? Has He pulled you away from the company of friends or classmates? He may have a torch to place in your hand. He may have something important to convey and may be asking that you step apart and attend. Are you willing to be instructed? When you become visible again to others—like a green shoot breaking through dark soil, like a torch breaking through a dark night—something will brighten in their hearts. Because though they may be chattering and having fun, they also are waiting. They are scanning the dark hoping for just such a sight. They are watching for the light you will bring.

> With you in His circle,
> Laura

Giver of life, of light, ever before us, whose Word is our lamp, how You shine! Amen.

ABOUT THE AUTHOR

LAURA GORDON GEORGAKAKOS is an editor and writer who has collaborated on books for Harcourt Brace, Sierra Club, Zondervan, DK Publishing, HarperCollins West and others. She has written a memoir, *The Words We left Unsaid*, and is the co-author of *Wild Discovery* for The Discovery Channel and *Billy Graham: God's Ambassador* for Time-Life Books. She received her B.A. (Phi Beta Kappa) in American Literature and M.A. in American Studies. A popular conference and retreat speaker, Laura joined the leadership of Community Bible Study in 2004 and currently serves as Teaching Director for the La Jolla, California class. She and her husband, Kosta, have been married since 1984, and live in Southern California.